IMAGES
of America

SAN LEANDRO

LOTTIE BEST. Manufacturing entrepreneur Daniel Best's daughter represents the Goddess of Liberty for an 1892 Independence Day celebration. (San Leandro Historical Photograph and Document Collection [SLHPDC] #1508.)

ON THE COVER: Dairymen get ready to milk the cows at the Phillips's Dairy, located in west San Leandro near First Avenue (today's Marina Boulevard), around 1915. (SLHPDC #68.)

IMAGES
of America

SAN LEANDRO

Cynthia Vrilakas Simons

ARCADIA
PUBLISHING

Published by Arcadia Publishing
Charleston, South Carolina

Library of Congress Catalog Card Number: 2008921580

For all general information contact Arcadia Publishing at:
Telephone 843-853-2070
Fax 843-853-0044
E-mail sales@arcadiapublishing.com
For customer service and orders:
Toll-Free 1-888-313-2665

Visit us on the Internet at www.arcadiapublishing.com

To my parents, Bob and Jane Vrilakas,
whose stories about Greek immigrants
and Oregon Trail pioneer ancestors
inspired my interest in history.

CONTENTS

ACKNOWLEDGMENTS

All the photographs in this book with an SLHPDC (San Leandro Historical Photograph and Document Collection) number are courtesy of the San Leandro Public Library. This book would not have been possible without this collection. I am grateful for its use and for volunteers Terry Galloway, Walter B. Peterson, Andy Galvan, and the other members of the historical photograph committee who collected, reproduced, indexed, and organized these photographs in preparation for San Leandro's 1972 centennial.

The outpouring of historical interest that accompanied San Leandro's 100th birthday was remarkable. Publications from this time include Harry E. Shaffer's San Leandro history book entitled *A Garden Grows in Eden*, Brent Galloway's *A San Leandro Centennial Album*, and the *San Leandro Recollections* (a series of pamphlets and oral histories). The video *There Was a Beginning* was also produced for the centennial, and a committee microfilmed San Leandro newspapers from the Bancroft Library to provide the San Leandro Public Library with a complete collection of local news. All of these sources contributed to this book.

San Leandro History Museum staff Addie Silveira and Mary Beth Barloga provided invaluable assistance with museum collections, fact-checking, and editing. Librarians Mary Lee Barr and Janet Prince answered many questions. Barr's *A Timeline of San Leandro History* and binders of articles and clippings provided a wealth of information. I do not wish to imagine what this manuscript would have been without the expert editing of my son Eric Simons.

I am grateful to former mayor Jack Maltester, Mayor Tony Santos, and Vice-Mayor Surlene Grant for taking time from their busy schedules to answer my questions. More people than I have space to acknowledge responded to my requests for photographs. These generous and wonderful people are a treasure. The chance to listen to their stories and share their photographs is an experience I will never forget.

INTRODUCTION

Geese and ducks attracted the first squatters to Rancho San Leandro. José Joaquin Estudillo's cattle ranch on the plain between San Francisco Bay and the East Bay hills had plentiful game, land seemingly for the taking, and a central location. San Leandro Creek, San Lorenzo Creek, and springs provided water. Squatter Thomas Mulford and many other forty-niners ignored the title claims of the Spanish, who had lived here for decades. Hunting wildfowl on Estudillo's land to sell in San Francisco, Mulford made enough money to build a bay landing and launch a freighting business, start a farm, develop a lucrative oyster fishery, and, many decades later, die a millionaire in San Leandro.

By the time Mulford died, Estudillo's ranch had been transformed into an American town. The Spanish who were here before Mulford developed cattle ranches where the native Californians had hunted and gathered in grasslands and oak forests. People who came after Mulford would replace cherry orchards and rhubarb fields with factories, suburban housing, and freeways. Ohlone village, Spanish *rancho,* the Cherry City, the City of Sunshine and Flowers, the Center of Industry—the area that is now San Leandro has had many identities. People have lived here for centuries, taking advantage of the bountiful resources, mild climate, and excellent location with bay access that would then attract new people, who created new communities.

The first people reached San Francisco Bay thousands of years ago. They found acorns, seeds, roots, fish, and shellfish. Flocks of birds filled the sky and marshes. Grizzly bears, elk, antelope, and small game were plentiful. The Jalquin and Yrgin people who lived in the San Leandro area were two of the approximately 40 independent small tribes referred to today collectively as the Ohlone. They developed an extensive and detailed knowledge of their environment, and they used controlled burns and other techniques to increase yields of plants and animals. A complex spirituality defined their relationship to each other and to their world.

Capt. Pedro Fages led a small expedition from Monterey through the East Bay in 1772, which was the first Spanish contact with the Jalquin and Yrgin. Spain decided to establish a presence in California (a colony she had claimed but ignored since 1542) beginning with Fr. Junípero Serra's Sacred Expedition in 1769. The Spanish newcomers were seeking souls, and they wanted to settle Alta (upper) California to keep it from other colonial empires. During the next several decades, 21 missions and a handful of presidios and pueblos dotted the California coast. Spanish colonization had unintended but devastating consequences for the Ohlone.

The *Californios* (Spanish colonists and their descendants) found grasslands, coastal access, and a climate that allowed them to raise thousands of cattle for hides and tallow, which were traded for goods brought by ship from the United States and elsewhere. Spanish and then Mexican colonial governors of California, after Mexico won independence and California became a Mexican colony, gave great tracts of land to settlers. The town of San Leandro developed over two of these land grants. Luís Maria Peralta's Rancho San Antonio stretched from San Leandro Creek north to El Cerrito Creek. José Joaquin Estudillo was given the area from San Leandro Creek south to San Lorenzo Creek. San Leandro gets its name from Estudillo's Rancho

San Leandro, which in turn took its name from El Rodeo de San Leandro, Mission San José's cattle round up area, named for Saint Leander, a sixth-century Spanish bishop. Beginning with Mission San José herds in 1797, thousands of cattle roamed the East Bay and were tended by Ohlone and Mexican *vaqueros* (cowboys).

Mexico ceded California to the United States in 1848 after the Mexican-American War. Any chance for a leisurely transition from Mexican ranching to American farms and towns was lost when the world rushed in after the discovery of gold in the same year. Thomas Mulford and his partners began the incursion onto Estudillo's land, but there were soon so many squatters along San Lorenzo Creek that the area was called Squatterville. The squatters, like the native people and the Spanish, found that plentiful game, land, and a golden climate suited their needs. Despite significant financial losses fighting in American courts to confirm their land titles, the Estudillos and Peraltas and their descendants were active participants in the new town.

As the town grew, it gained regional importance from its central location. For a brief period, San Leandro won the political tug-of-war between towns that wanted to be the seat of Alameda County. As the county seat from 1855 until 1873, San Leandro was the bustling center of East Bay politics. After the county seat was transferred to Oakland, San Leandro veered onto a quieter path.

Farmers discovered that they could grow almost anything on San Leandro's fertile flatlands, while bay access and early railroads provided the means to ship to state and national markets. Dairy farms, chicken ranches, wheat fields, and acres of vegetables flourished, but orchards covered most of the land. In 1909, to celebrate a bumper crop of cherries, the town decided to hold a cherry festival and established the community as the Cherry City. San Leandro still honors the past with cherry festivals today.

Many of San Leandro's early settlers were from the Azores. The large Portuguese population in the late 19th and early 20th centuries earned San Leandro the moniker "the Portuguese Capital of the West."

Industrialists in the late 19th century came to San Leandro because farmers needed agricultural equipment for clay soil and vast acreages, and there were rail lines to ship their products elsewhere. San Leandro had factories producing tractors, combines, hay presses, and other equipment geared to the needs of farmers, as well as a cannery to preserve their produce by the late 1800s. Still San Leandro was the Cherry City until the 1930s, when floriculture began to replace farm fields and the town began to call itself the City of Sunshine and Flowers.

World War II military industries in the Bay Area offered employment to people still suffering the effects of the Great Depression. During the war years, thousands immigrated here from across America, and the population continued to swell in the 1950s and 1960s. Many farm fields were sold to developers, who built housing for those new arrivals. Annexation of surrounding fields for industrial development, coupled with multiplying subdivisions, completed the transition from orchards to suburb. San Leandro left behind the "sunshine-and-flowers" identity and began billing itself as the "City of Industry."

At first, the opportunities to take part in this expanding suburb were not equally extended. Housing discrimination excluded many, particularly African Americans and Asian Americans. Once California's Rumford Fair Housing Act was able to take effect, San Leandro experienced its most recent transformation into one of the most diverse cities in one of the most diverse states in the nation.

The elk and grizzlies, the vast cattle ranches, and the cherry orchards are gone. Today the land is covered mostly with housing for San Leandro's greatest resource—its people. Flowers blooming in the fertile soil of their yards, San Leandrans live between the sparkling bay and gentle hills, creating a new city to unite their many cultures and talents.

One

First People and Spanish Transformation
Precontact to 1849

About 1,500 years ago, the Ohlone replaced an earlier Bay Area people. The Ohlone were not one nation but were instead comprised of about 40 independent tribelets, or village communities, in the Bay Area and as far south as Monterey. San Leandro was the home of the Jalquin and Yrgin tribelets. The Spanish called all these communities the *Costeño*, coast people, which became the term Costanoan. In 1971, descendants adopted "Ohlone" to replace the Spanish term. The Ohlone were hunters and gatherers who moved from permanent villages to temporary camps to take advantage of seasonal foods. Each tribelet hunted and gathered within a well-defined territory but intermarried and traded with other groups.

Mission Dolores in San Francisco (established 1776) and Mission San José (established 1797) attracted and coerced the Ohlone to join. The missions were intended to convert the native people to Roman Catholicism and teach them how to live as Spanish citizens. A terrible death rate, as high as 75 percent, resulted from epidemics of disease in the missions. In addition, the introduction of cattle, sheep, pigs, and invasive seeds displaced traditional Ohlone food sources.

Teen-aged Luís María Peralta and his parents came to California with an expedition in 1775–1776 led by Juan Bautista de Anza. In 1820, the last Spanish governor rewarded Peralta's long military career with a vast East Bay land grant from San Leandro Creek to El Cerrito Creek. After Mexico achieved independence from Spain, the missions were closed, and their lands were distributed as land grants. The first Mexican Alta California governor awarded Mission San José's northern area to retired soldier José Joaquin Estudillo.

Former mission Indians and new recruits went to work for the *rancheros* (ranchers). The colony gave rise to an elite culture often remembered for its romantic fandango and fiestas, skilled horsemanship, and legendary hospitality. Laborers, however, usually received nothing more than food, shelter, and clothing, and were essentially bound to the ranchero. An economy based entirely on the hide-and-tallow trade—with little in the way of commerce, manufacturing, or an educational system—kept the system in place until the arrival of the Americans.

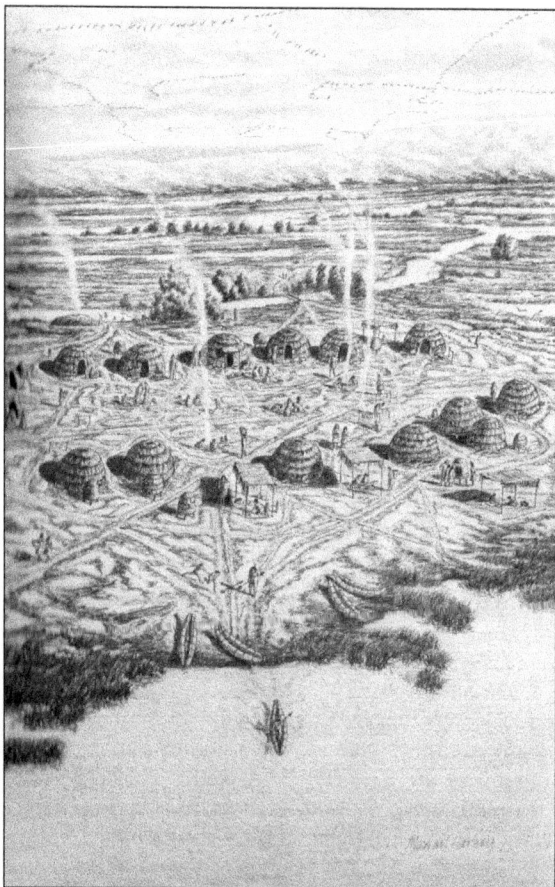

OHLONE LIFE. The largest native village in the San Leandro area was at a natural spring near today's Fairmont Hospital. These illustrations by Michael Harney show village and hunting scenes. People in the village go about their tasks, preparing food, weaving baskets, or leaching and pounding acorns that would be baked into bread or made into mush. Two women return carrying gathering baskets, perhaps filled with roots, seeds, or acorns. A man paddles a boat made from tule. Smoke is rising from cooking fires and from a *temescal* (sweat lodge) down by the creek. Below, a man snares birds attracted by his straw-stuffed decoys. Men hunted deer, elk, bears, small mammals, and birds, and caught fish from the creek and bay. (Both, *The Ohlone Way* by Malcolm Margolin, Heyday Books.)

10

DANCE OF INDIANS AT MISSION SAN JOSÉ. Georg Heinrich Langsdorff drew this image *c.* 1805 of painted Ohlone dancers. Dance was an important means of expression, social interaction, and religious ceremony. There were dances to honor spirits, prepare for war, celebrate ripening acorns, and many other facets of life. A chorus of singers chanted and kept rhythm with split-stick rattles. (Bancroft Library.)

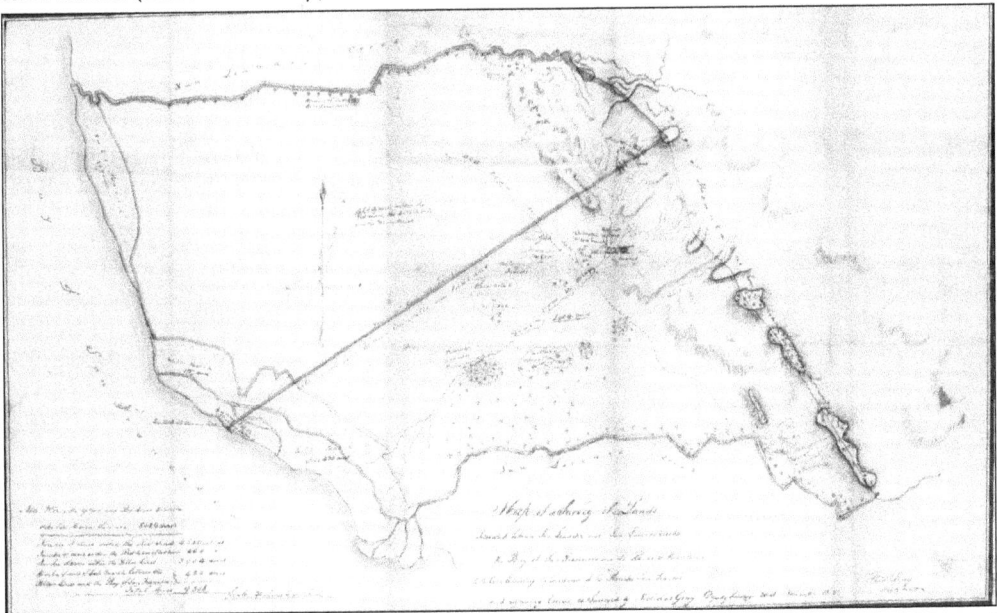

SURVEY OF RANCHO SAN LEANDRO, 1855. When the missions closed, some Ohlone returned to live at their village site. Estudillo's grant mentioned the American Indians living "by the drainage of the springs," and the grant excluded "the lands cultivated by the above-mentioned Indians." The diagonal line through the middle of the map separates the Ohlone area on the southern section of Rancho San Leandro. (Bancroft Library.)

11

HISTORICAL MAP OF THE EAST BAY. This map from the National Park Service illustrates the Spanish and Mexican land grants of the East Bay. San Leandro developed over two land grants. North of San Leandro Creek, the 44,800-acre Rancho San Antonio was awarded to Luís María Peralta in 1820. South of the creek, the 7,010-acre Rancho San Leandro was awarded to José Joaquin Estudillo in 1842. Note the major road running from the right edge through Ranchos San Lorenzo, San Leandro, San Antonio, San Pablo, and into El Pinole. The earliest Spanish explorers remarked on the "well-beaten paths" of the native people. Mission San José used and developed this path to reach the *embarcaderos* and adobes of the rancheros, making it a part of El Camino Real, the "royal highway" of public roads that connected missions and settlements. Today's Mission Boulevard in Fremont and Hayward, East Fourteenth Street in San Leandro, and International Boulevard in Oakland, roughly follow the route of this ancient path. (San Leandro Museum.)

JOSÉ JOAQUIN AND JUANA ESTUDILLO. Joaquin was born in Monterey in 1800. He joined the military when he was 15 and married Juana del Carmen Martinez in 1823. They settled on Rancho San Leandro in 1837. The grant was confirmed in 1842, though its vague boundaries caused problems between Joaquin and his neighbor Castro. Juana's dowry of 300 white cattle from her father's Rancho Pinole started the San Leandro herd. More than 100 Ohlone and Mexican vaqueros and servants did the ranch and housework. The spring roundup (rodeo) of the freely roaming cattle allowed each ranchero to separate his animals and brand the calves. Families gathered and celebrated with several days of dancing, cockfighting, gambling, horse races, and bull or bull-and-bear fights. After the slaughter, the hides and tallow were stored to wait for the arrival of the next coastal trader. (Both, Bancroft Library.)

13

WILLIAM HEATH DAVIS AND MARÍA DE JESUS ESTUDILLO DAVIS. Davis Street is named for this son of a Boston seafarer and American Hawaiian mother. His work as a clerk and supercargo (ship's agent) in Mexican California brought him into contact with *Californio* families. He fell in love with Estudillo's daughter María, and they were married at Mission Dolores in 1847. He and his brother-in-law John Ward, who married María's sister Concepción, managed most of the Estudillo family business after Joaquin's death in 1852. Davis and Ward were instrumental in San Leandro's inception. They negotiated with squatters on Estudillo's behalf, got Juana to donate land for the county and city, and lobbied for San Leandro to be the Alameda County seat. (Left, SLHPDC #103; below, Bancroft Library.)

DAVIS MEMOIR. These illustrations are from Davis's book about his life in Mexican California and then during California's transition to an American state, including his years living in Yerba Buena, his marriage, his founding of "New Town" in San Diego, and his final years in Oakland, struggling for financial security. Above, a bridal party accompanies the bride, who is riding a "spirited jet black horse" to her wedding. Noted for their riding skills, *Californio* women often preferred to travel by horseback rather than via the awkward *carreta* (a two-wheeled oxcart). Below is an illustration of an incident Davis titled "Author's Grizzled Hairs Due to Grizzly Bears." Davis described camping out on Rancho San Antonio when, unbeknownst to him, the Peraltas were hunting bear nearby. Grizzlies terrorized him for most of the night. (Both, *Seventy-Five Years in California* by William Heath Davis, J. Howell Publishing.)

MEXICAN VAQUERO. Western artist Edward Borein (1873–1945) depicts the skilled cowboy of Alta California in this 1915 etching. The vaquero lived in the saddle. He and his horse developed the lightning-quick responses necessary to herd, brand, and round up thousands of cattle. Borein was born in San Leandro and remembered cattle drives through the town. (Fine Arts Museums of San Francisco, California State Library loan.)

WARD FAMILY. Concepción, the oldest Estudillo daughter, married John Ward, an Irishman who came to California in 1840 as a cabin boy and returned during the Gold Rush. He and Davis laid out the town on February 27, 1855. Ward was involved in many projects, including building a gristmill and encouraging logging of the redwood trees at upper San Leandro Creek. (Casa Peralta.)

ESTUDILLO HOME. The high price of beef during the Gold Rush gained Joaquin and Juana Estudillo enough of a fortune to build this grand home in 1850. After their deaths, their daughter Magdalena lived here with her husband John Nugent, publisher of the *San Francisco Herald*. (His newspaper went bankrupt after he denounced the Vigilance Committee.) The home was razed in 1947 to build St. Leander's rectory. (SLHPDC #105.)

YGNACIO PERALTA. Luís María Peralta's four sons, Antonio, José Domingo, Vicente, and Ygnacio, split up and settled his Rancho San Antonio. In 1842, after he retired as a soldier and *alcalde* (mayor-judge) of San José, Ygnacio built an adobe on the north bank of San Leandro Creek. The ranch eventually supported about 7,000 cattle and 2,000 horses. (Oil painting by Quince Galloway, courtesy Casa Peralta.)

PERALTA HOME, ALTA MIRA CLUB. The Peraltas built and elegantly furnished this brick home on Lafayette Avenue in 1860, giving their old adobe to their son. The people on the porch are probably Ygnacio and his wife, Rafaela. Several of their descendants played a significant role in the new town of San Leandro. The beautiful home is now the Alta Mira Club. (SLHPDC #4.)

MARÍA ANTONIA PERALTA. Ygnacio's and Rafaela's daughter María married William Pinkney Toler in 1853. William raised the American flag twice at Monterey, first when Commodore Thomas ap Catesby Jones prematurely seized the Mexican California capital and again after the Bear Flag Revolt. María was a Spanish-court debutante and attended the inaugural ball of U.S. president James Buchanan. As a widow, she lived in the home that is now the Casa Peralta. (SLHPDC #1680.)

Two

SQUATTERVILLE AND
A NEW TOWN
1849 TO 1900

In 1848, California became a territory of the United States and gold was discovered. Gold fever precipitated the migration of hundreds of thousands of people from all over the world. Many forty-niner gold seekers found it more profitable to make money off the other miners instead.

Although the treaty between Mexico and the United States protected Mexican land rights, the rancheros were required to prove title in American courts, which was a long and costly process. Meanwhile, newcomers took advantage of the confusion and moved onto Estudillo's and Peralta's land. Many of the squatters became prominent citizens in early San Leandro.

In 1853, the California legislature created Alameda County out of a portion of Contra Costa County and established the first county seat in New Haven. The location of the county seat was a point of contention, so an election was held in 1854. San Leandro won the election, although it took an act of the legislature in 1856 to settle allegations of voter fraud and designate San Leandro as the new county seat.

The town of San Leandro began when Juana Estudillo donated 200 acres of land to establish a town site. Her sons-in-law William Heath Davis and John Ward constructed buildings in the area that would soon be San Leandro Plaza. Hotels, saloons, businesses, churches, and schools joined the landscape. Cattle ranching gave way to a growing American town, with surrounding farms.

San Leandro incorporated on March 21, 1872. The vibrant community boasted a railroad and two bay landings for transportation, which attracted farmers and industrialists. Oysters were the most valuable fishery in California toward the end of the 19th century, and oyster farms soon filled most of the shoreline.

In 1868, a major earthquake on the Hayward fault destroyed the San Leandro county courthouse. Oakland promoters began lobbying for a new county seat, and an election in 1873 transferred that status to the much-larger Oakland. San Leandro, the center of county political life for almost 20 years, began forging a new identity as an agricultural and industrial center.

THOMAS W. MULFORD. Barely 20 years old when he left New York and came to California in 1849, Mulford and his partners found wealth not by finding gold, but by rowing a whaleboat across the bay to hunt wildfowl on Rancho San Leandro to sell in San Francisco. They soon built a landing and established a freighting business, shipping as many as 1,000 birds to market a month. (SLHPDC #2095.)

MULFORD'S LANDING. Mulford is standing just right of the aft mast in his schooner *c.* 1900. Before railroads, landings were an essential element of transportation, and scow schooners crisscrossed the bay with hay, produce, game, and other goods. San Leandro products could be shipped from Mulford's Landing (called Wick's Landing until Mulford bought out his partner) at today's marina area or Robert's Landing at San Lorenzo Creek. (SLHPDC #620.)

MULFORD FARM, C. 1890. Mulford expanded into several other ventures. He was a manager of the Estudillo House, developed an oyster fishery, and established a 350-acre farm and dairy ranch called Shore Acres on land he eventually bought from Estudillo. When he died in 1907, Mulford left his estate, worth $2 million, to his daughter and son-in-law, Gertrude and Robert Collins. (SLHPDC #39.)

MULFORD GARDENS. Mulford's granddaughter Ruth Collins plays on an oyster-shell path at Shore Acres in 1908. Her parents continued to operate the dairy after Mulford's death, but the end of an era came in 1924 when the cattle had to be slaughtered because of hoof-and-mouth disease. The land was sold, and the Mulford Gardens subdivision began in 1927. It was annexed to San Leandro in 1957. (SLHPDC #1188.)

ESTUDILLO HOUSE. The transition from Mexican ranch to American town began when John Ward and William H. Davis constructed the Estudillo House, an elegant hotel and restaurant, in 1855. The stagecoach stop, and later the streetcar stop, was in front of this hotel on San Leandro Plaza. It even served ferry passengers because of a plank road, Ward Street, which was built from here to the San Lorenzo wharf. (San Leandro Museum.)

SAN LEANDRO PLAZA. The intersection of three roads, East Fourteenth Street, Washington Avenue, and Estudillo Avenue, which were then called Haywards Road, Watkins Street, and Ward Street, respectively, formed the plaza triangle at the heart of the new town. This view, taken around 1880, shows hotels, a blacksmith shop, a general store along Haywards Road, Gorman's Saloon with kegs on the awning, and a real estate office along Ward. (SLHPDC #891.)

22

ROBERT'S LANDING. Squatter William Roberts, paralleling Mulford's ventures, hunted wildfowl on Estudillo's property to sell in San Francisco. This illustration from the 1878 Thompson and West *Official and Historical Atlas Map of Alameda County* shows his landing and freight warehouses. He had an oyster farm as well. His home was moved from its original location and now stands on Lewelling Boulevard. (SLHPDC #3.)

WEBBER HOUSE. This hotel on Clarke Street, located across the street from the courthouse, was owned and managed by Mary Hawkins Webber. She and her first husband, R. Tomlinson Hawkins, who died on the way to join the Union Army, had a farm in the valley that is now Lake Chabot. She owned and operated the Webber House from the time her second husband, Charles Webber, died in 1864 until her death in 1915. (SLHPDC #94.)

COUNTY COURTHOUSE. Davis and Ward secured land from Juana Estudillo for the courthouse and then rode up and down the county to lobby voters for San Leandro as the county seat. The two-story, neoclassical-style courthouse is shown here soon after it was built in 1856. It occupied the site of present-day St. Leander's School, on the corner of Davis and Clarke Streets. (SLHPDC #1.)

COURTHOUSE STEPS, 1866. On the far left is Alameda County sheriff and famous lawman Harry Morse. He captured Black Bart, among other exploits. Band members from left to right are Jerome Moore, Alfred Crane, J. M. Costigan, George B. Standeford (*Alameda County Gazette* editor), L. J. Bullard, Deputy Sheriff P. R. Borein (father of Western artist Edward Borein), Deputy County Clerk J. W. Josselyn, and George Chase. (SLHPDC #522.)

EARTHQUAKE. Early in the morning on October 21, 1868, a major earthquake shook the Hayward fault. The courthouse building (above) and the San Francisco and Alameda Railroad depot in Hayward (below) were destroyed. Damage in the East Bay was extensive. Thirty people were killed, including J. W. Josselyn, a deputy county clerk who tried to escape through the courthouse door (he is one of the band members in the preceding photograph). Deputy Sheriff Borein was tossed out of bed. He escaped by climbing out a window but left the keys to the jail behind. Prisoners trapped in the basement jail were eventually rescued and transferred to Oakland. The nearby First Methodist Church was used as a temporary courthouse while makeshift repairs were made. (Above, SLHPDC #817; below, Hayward Area Historical Society.)

FIRST SCHOOL. At the petition of San Leandro parents, a school district for San Leandro, Union School District No. 1 of Alameda County, was established in 1856. The Union School was built at the corner of Clarke and Hepburn (today's West Joaquin) Streets, and school began in December 1856. By 1872, the school had four teachers with about 50 pupils each, and a special tax paid for a new addition. A second addition, a separate building called the Annex, was built in 1885. In the 1899 photograph below, pupils and teachers pose in front of the Annex in the foreground, and the old school building with the addition is in back. The district reorganized as the San Leandro School District of Alameda County in 1906. (Above, SLHPDC #838; below, SLHPDC #40.)

RAILROADS. The San Francisco and Alameda Railroad (SF&ARR) reached San Leandro in 1865, with a line from Hayward to Alameda and ferry service across the bay. Pictured above is the SF&ARR engine *J. G. Kellogg.* Central Pacific, through its subsidiary Western Pacific, acquired the SF&ARR and laid a line to Sacramento, which brought the first transcontinental train through San Leandro in 1869. San Leandro was on the transcontinental railroad line until the late 1870s, when a new line through Carquinez bypassed San Leandro. Southern Pacific then acquired Central Pacific and continued to operate, expand, and improve East Bay lines. The depot moved to Davis Street; not coincidentally, industrial development in San Leandro began along the rail line. Pictured below, men are laying railroad tracks through San Leandro. (Above, SLHPDC #1277; below, SLHPDC #362.)

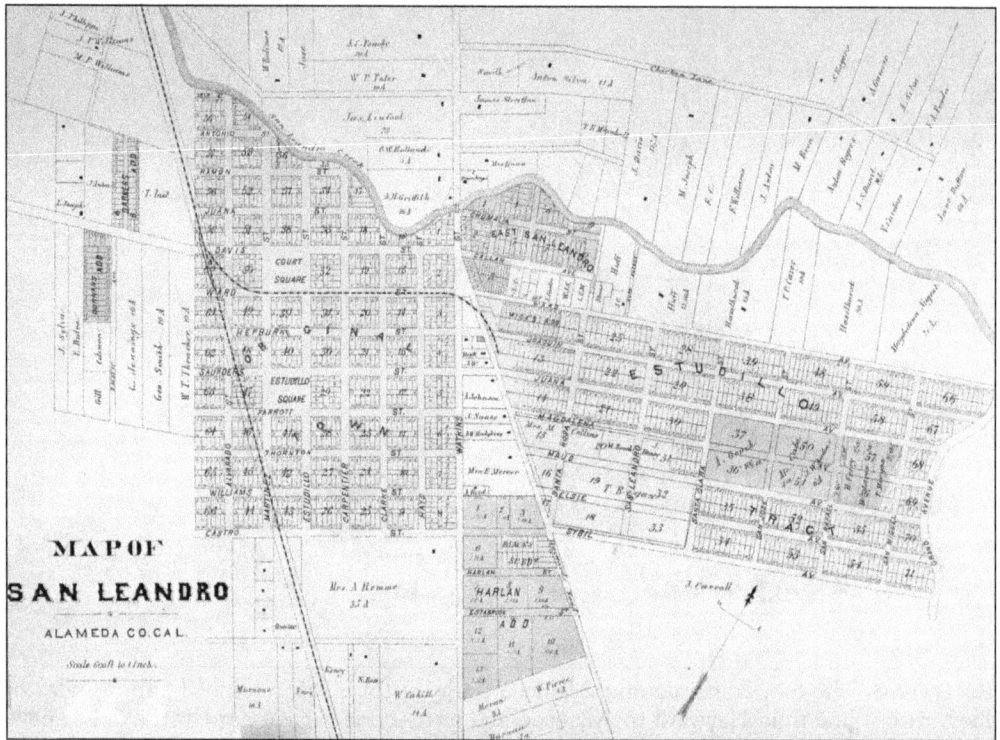

SAN LEANDRO MAP. This map from the 1878 Thompson and West *Official and Historical Atlas Map of Alameda County* shows the small town surrounded by farms. Watkins Street (today's Washington Avenue) and Haywards Road (today's East Fourteenth Street) meet at the Plaza. Chicken Lane (today's Dutton Avenue) runs horizontally at the top right, and Ward Street (today's Estudillo Avenue) runs horizontally through the center. (SLHPDC #1060.)

TOWN HALL AND DAVIS STREET. The building with the cupola in the left center is the old town hall on the north side of Davis Street between East Fourteenth and Hays Streets. It was built in 1876 at a cost of $500 in gold and $200 in silver, and served as the city government center until the new city hall opened on East Fourteenth Street in 1939. (SLHPDC #661.)

ROBERT AND HENRIETTA FARRELLY HOMES. Another Gold Rush squatter, Robert Farrelly emigrated from Pennsylvania. Pictured above is a drawing of Farrelly's showplace home and orchard from the 1878 Thompson and West atlas. Robert served as county treasurer, county supervisor, and San Leandro school trustee, and he was an organizer and director of the Bank of San Leandro. In the years after Robert's death, Henrietta built an imposing new home (shown below) and took on a major role as town benefactor. She established the first Boys' Club in San Leandro, provided a building for the American Legion, and donated funds to initiate the San Leandro Grammar School Band and pay its director, Charles Way. After she died in 1927, her will provided $50,000 to the Alameda County Foundation and money to build the Farrelly Pool. (Above, SLHPDC #1056; below, SLHPDC #1711.)

SOCRATES HUFF AND THE HUFF HOME. San Leandro pioneer Huff came to California from Michigan in 1849. He lived in San Leandro from 1859 until his death in 1907. He served as the Alameda County tax collector and treasurer and as a San Leandro trustee. He was a San Leandro Plow Company director and had a freighting business, a farm, and oyster beds, but banking was his main occupation. He and his wife, Amelia, had seven daughters. Their beautiful home was one of the few illustrated in the 1878 Thompson and West atlas. Surrounded with orchards and gardens, the estate featured a carriage driveway, a fountain, and a stone fence made from lava imported from Mount Fujiyama. The estate was located where the fire station at the corner of Huff and Estudillo Avenues is today. (Left, SLHPDC #1964; below, SLHPDC #1954.)

CHABOT RESERVOIR. French Canadian Anthony Chabot mined for gold by using a hose to wash dirt and gravel into a sluice box, an idea picked up by another miner, who added a nozzle and created the destructive hydraulic mining technique that blasted away hillsides. After building other water projects in the area, Chabot organized the Contra Costa Water Works to supply water to Oakland. He built Temescal Dam first, then planned and oversaw the construction of a dam on San Leandro Creek beginning in 1874. Layers of compacted clay filled the foundation pit and rose up the canyon to form the puddle wall. Dynamite charges blasted dirt and gravel into flumes far back into the valley. High-pressure hoses then washed the material onto the puddle wall to create the earth-filled dam. (Right, Oakland Public Library; below, CSU East Bay Anthropology Department.)

YEMA-PO. Chabot hired as many as 800 Chinese laborers to construct the dam. Prof. George Miller of California State University, Hayward, led a 1981 archaeological excavation of the laborers' camp. It was called *Yema-Po*, Chinese for wild horse slope, because of the horses driven back and forth to compact the clay layers. This enormous wok was one of the 60,000 artifacts uncovered. (CSU East Bay Anthropology Department.)

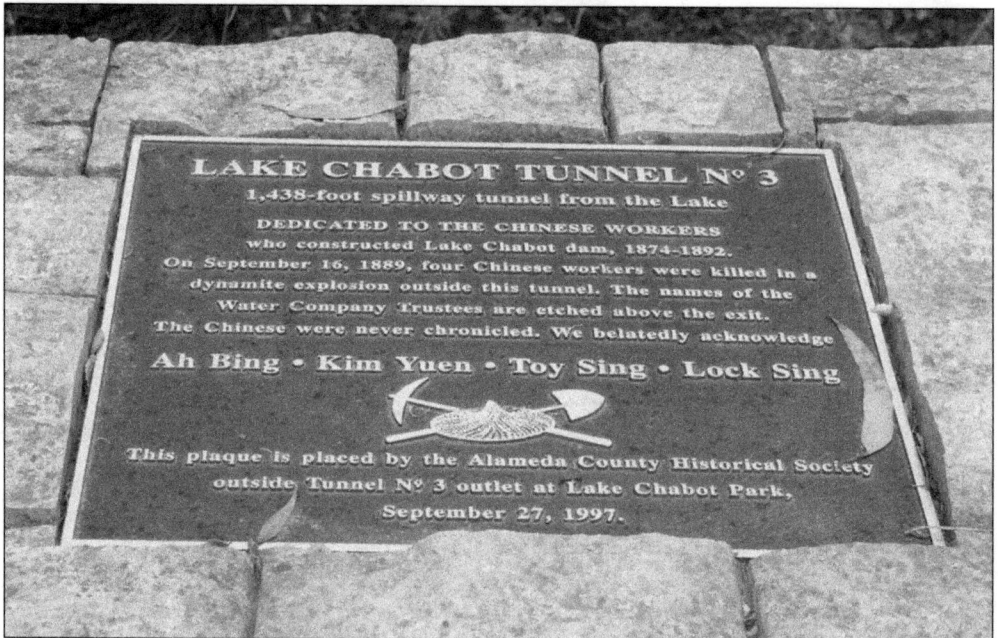

TRAGEDY AT TUNNEL NO. 3. A night crew in 1889 was excavating a trench from a dam tunnel to the creek when a blasting cartridge exploded, killing four men, who are now honored with this plaque placed by the Alameda County Historical Society. Little was known about the Chinese construction crew until research by Jacqueline Beggs and Miller's archaeological dig uncovered details about their lives. (Devon Weston.)

32

LAKE CHABOT AND THE CREEK, 1948. San Leandro Creek runs its course from headwaters near Sibley Volcanic Park through Upper San Leandro and Chabot Reservoirs, through San Leandro, and into the bay at Arrowhead Marsh. The creek has provided salt (an Ohlone trading resource) from the marshes at its mouth, redwood trees logged from the upper creek area, fish, recreation, and, of course, water. In 1855, a man caught a beautifully colored fish in the creek, which the California Academy of Sciences described as a new species, called rainbow trout. For almost a century, scientists thought the rainbow was discovered here first, until Oregon claimed the honors for the Columbia River when a 20th-century researcher found a description of a rainbow trout caught there in 1836. Below, the Huff family picnics on the banks of the creek. (Above, SLHPDC #764; below, Judy Downing.)

FIRE DEPARTMENT. The first official fire company, Union Hose Company No. 1, was organized in 1876 and was housed in the town hall. They fought fires with bucket brigades until a hose cart (pictured above) was added in 1887. After some San Leandro firefighters fell from exhaustion while pulling a heavy water wagon and hose cart to a fire (the Oakland company had to put out the fire), the fire chief's complaints to town trustees finally got the company a horse as well. Photographed at left, listed from left to right, are Walter Stratton, Chief ? Cannon, and Francis Frates in 1876. Cannon holds a silver trumpet megaphone, which was presented to the fire department by the Home Mutual Insurance Company in 1876. It is still a proud possession of the fire department today. (Both, Ray Jannson.)

SAN LEANDRO PLAZA, 1885. In this view of the downtown looking south, part of the Estudillo House is visible on the right edge. Watkins Street (today's Washington Avenue) angles off to the right, and Haywards Road (today's East Fourteenth Street) angles off to the left. (SLHPDC #2101.)

ELECTRIC RAILWAY. The Oakland, San Leandro, and Haywards Electric Railway train stops at the Plaza on opening day, May 7, 1892. People could live farther from work and shops with this technological advance in public transportation—no more bone-jarring, dusty, or bogged-down-in-the-mud stagecoach journeys. The line ran 14.3 miles from Oakland to Haywards (Haywards dropped the "s" in 1911 to become Hayward). (SLHPDC #324.)

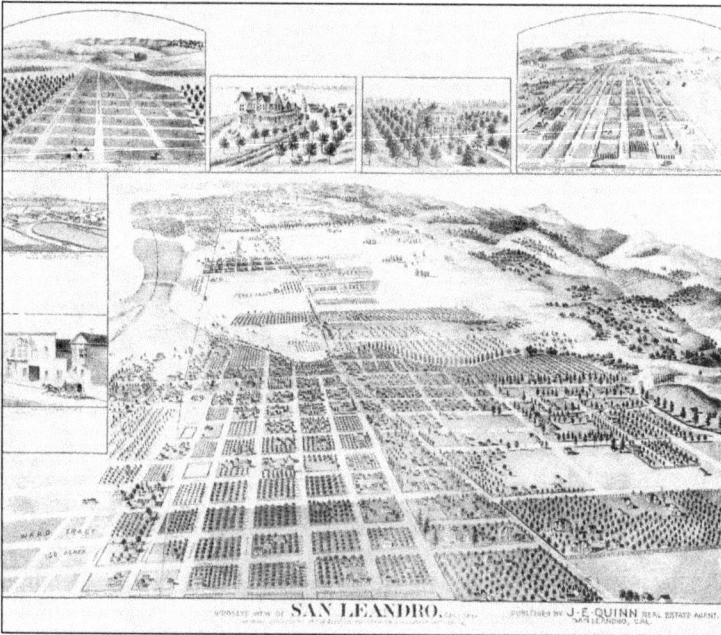

BIRDS-EYE MAP. A real estate agent published this birds-eye view map in 1892, the same year that the electric railway was completed. Orchards and farm fields cover most of the land, but subdivisions would soon spring up along the rail line. What could be more enticing for prospective home buyers than country living with convenient public transportation? (San Leandro Library.)

FIRST METHODIST CHURCH AND SARMENTO'S. The first church in San Leandro was built in 1856 on Hays Street, shown in the photograph above in 1897. Next door, George Sarmento stands in the doorway of his blacksmith shop. The Methodist Church later moved to a new building on Bancroft Avenue. The blacksmith shop building and Sarmento home around the corner at 308 West Joaquin Avenue are still standing. (SLHPDC #850.)

36

St. Leander's Catholic Church. This building was completed in 1864; its 96-foot-tall spire is visible in many old photographs. Juana Estudillo donated the land, and Rafaela Peralta donated a bell that Vicente Peralta had imported from Spain and had been used in his private chapel at Temescal. The building was razed in 1957 for the construction of St. Leander's primary school. A new church was built across West Estudillo Avenue. (SLHPDC #1975.)

St. Mary's School. Students pose with Fr. William G. O'Mahony. St. Leander's bought the old county courthouse building and converted it into a school. In 1881, six Dominican sisters began teaching a grammar and high school course for girls. Boys began attending the school two years later. After new construction, the school was renamed St. Leander's in 1955. (Jackie Hayes.)

FIRST PRESBYTERIAN CHURCH. Built in 1867 at Clarke and Hepburn Streets, the main building was moved to Ashland around 1928. The north wing (right side of building in this picture) remained and was used as a missionary school. Slated for demolition, it was saved by the San Leandro Historical Society (SLHS) and was moved behind the Casa Peralta. It is now the SLHS headquarters, affectionately called "the Little Brown Church." (SLHPDC #558.)

LITTLE SHUL. The San Leandro Hebrew Congregation incorporated in 1886. The congregation built a synagogue, called the Little Shul, on Chumalia Street in 1889. The Little Shul was sold after a new Temple Beth Sholom was built on Dolores Street in the 1940s. In 1970, the congregation bought the building back and moved it behind the temple, where it is again used for services and classes. (SLHPDC #1854.)

BLACKSMITH. Fred Federighi Sr., Monte Federighi, Charlie Grazzini, and "Pongi" Toti are four of the five men in this photograph of Federighi's Blacksmith Shop in 1906. Blacksmiths made horseshoes, wheels, farm implements, household wares, and even manufactured agricultural equipment. (SLHPDC #535.)

SAN LEANDRO PLAZA. A streetcar stops at the Plaza in this turn-of-the-20th-century photograph. The new Herrscher buildings (with cupolas) flank Washington Avenue on the right, while another streetcar runs down East Fourteenth Street. (San Leandro Museum.)

MULFORD LANDING OYSTER SHEDS. Oyster beds lined much of the shoreline in the late 1800s, when oystering was the most valuable fishing enterprise in the state. Larger companies soon swallowed up smaller owners such as Mulford, Roberts, and Huff. The *San Leandro Reporter* wrote about a takeover: "On Saturday morning just as the sun peeped over the brown Castro Valley hills a low rakish sloop with a Gatling gun mounted on the poop deck and with a crew of hardy men armed to their back teeth sailed into the quiet and peaceful harbor of San Lorenzo and in the name of, it is presumed, the Shoalwater Oyster Co., took possession of some of the oyster beds just south of those operated by the San Leandro Oyster Co." (SLHPDC #2129.)

OYSTER BARGE. Jack London wrote stories about being an "oyster pirate" in his youth. The pirates snuck into East Bay oyster farms by boat at night to steal oysters. London later joined the Fish Patrol, whose job it was to catch the pirates. Look for the faint image of a man with a rifle on the far left, protecting the harvesters from turf wars or pirates. (SLHPDC #468.)

HARVESTING OYSTERS. After the transcontinental railroad was completed, fisheries began importing oyster spat from the East Coast. The spat, an early stage of the oyster, was set over existing beds to mature. The introduced species quickly overran the native Olympia oysters. Hydraulic mining debris and other pollution put an end to commercial oystering in San Francisco Bay early in the 20th century. (SLHPDC #2126.)

BRASS BAND. An 1885 photograph depicts San Leandro's first brass band. Before radio and electronic equipment, brass bands supplied party music, parade music, and entertainment. Pictured from left to right are (first row) John Garcia, Joe Calhoun, John Calhoun, Joe August, Manuel Bettencourt, Mark Halverson, Manuel Miller, Antone August, Manuel Crab, and Charles Cunha; (second row) Frank Calhoun, Manuel Foster, Frank Williams, Joseph Olimpia, Manuel J. Andrade, and Mike Victor. (SLHPDC #118.)

SPANISH-AMERICAN WAR. Townspeople and children gather to honor the troops, who are possibly part of divisions leaving for the Philippines. In the patriotic fervor after the outbreak of the war, Col. Frank S. Hastings donated a 165-foot flagpole (only the base is visible in this photograph) that was installed on the Plaza in 1897. (San Leandro Museum.)

Three

Whaling Ships and Azorean Sailors
Portuguese Capital of the West

The pressures of population and limited land in the 19th century pushed many young men in the Azores to emigrate. Whalers from Boston, stopping in the islands to recruit sailors, provided the means. Some Portuguese sailors seized the opportunity to jump ship or buy freedom in San Francisco during the Gold Rush, while others spent time in Hawaii or New England to work and save money for passage to California.

San Leandro's land attracted many Portuguese immigrants, who paid the high prices demanded by the first settlers, then made their dairy farms, chicken ranches, and truck farms successful with hard work and intensive farming techniques. A character in Jack London's novel *Valley of the Moon* remarks about San Leandro's Portuguese immigrants, "they worked mornin', noon, an' night, all hands, women an' kids. Because they could get more out of 20 acres than we could out of a hundred an' sixty . . . Not an inch wasted. Where we got one thin crop, they get four fat crops. An' look at the way they crowd it—currants between the tree rows, beans between the currant rows, a row of beans close on each side of the trees, an' rows of beans along the ends of the tree rows."

The Hawaiian sugar industry recruited many Portuguese workers in the 19th century. Political uncertainty and economic depression spurred many of those Portuguese to leave for California in the 1890s. Locals referred to Orchard Avenue, where many of the Hawaiian Portuguese settled, as Kanaka Lane, a term meaning native Hawaiian. By the 20th century, about two-thirds of San Leandro's population was Portuguese.

Love of family and reverence for religious celebrations brought Portuguese San Leandrans together. Portuguese traditions, such as Holy Ghost *festas* (festivals), took root and blossomed in San Leandro. Until the population boom after World War II, San Leandro was often called the Portuguese capital of the West. Today San Leandro's population is only about .04 percent Portuguese, but queens still carry the crown in the procession, and the savory smell of *sopas e carne* permeates the neighborhood during annual Holy Ghost festivals.

UPEC HEADQUARTERS. Portuguese immigrants established the *União Portuguesa do Estado da California* (UPEC), or Portuguese Union of the State of California, in San Leandro on August 1, 1880, to provide death benefits to members and to maintain Portuguese culture and language. Today San Leandro is still home to the UPEC, the oldest fraternal benefit society in California, which has subordinate councils throughout California and Nevada, and San Leandro is home to Council No. 1. (SLHPDC #135.)

UPEC OFFICERS, 1888. Officers in regalia pose in front of the town hall on Davis Street. From left to right are Carl Iversen, Joseph Bettencourt, Manuel Andrade, Manuel Rodgers, Jesse Woods, Joseph Olympia, Manuel Braga, Joe Barbara, and Manuel Avilla. (SLHPDC #176.)

MANUEL GARCIA. Nine-year-old Garcia, from the Azores, joined a whaling crew, jumped ship five years later, became a barber and dentist, and set up shop in San Leandro in the home pictured here on Chumalia Street. He was a town trustee and owned land on Sybil Avenue, where he grew cherries and other produce. His widow, Mary, continued working the land, which was one of the last orchards in town, until 1946. (SLHPDC #1868.)

PORTUGUESE BAND, 1880s. This Portuguese *filarmónica*, or marching band, poses with children dressed up for a celebration, perhaps a Holy Ghost parade. (UPEC.)

45

GREAT GILDERSLEEVE. The gifted comedic actor Harold Peary was born of Portuguese ancestry in San Leandro. He originated the character of the Great Gildersleeve on the radio show *Fibber McGee and Molly*. His popularity spurred the development of his own radio show in 1941. Throckmorton P. Gildersleeve entertained the nation not only on the radio, but also in four films. (Carlos Almeida and the San Leandro Museum.)

FOCHA FAMILY, 1911. Harold Peary is the little boy at the bottom of the steps in this photograph of the Focha family at their home on Dabner Street. The street was named for Peary's grandfather, John Pimentel Dabner (his name was anglicized from Davina after he emigrated from the Azores). John and María Dabner started the celebration of the Holy Ghost in San Leandro possibly as early as 1870. (SLHPDC #1920.)

IDES. The first San Leandro *Irmandade do Divino Espírito Santo* (IDES), or the Brotherhood of the Divine Holy Spirit, was founded in 1882 with Joseph Focha, son-in-law of John and María Dabner, as its first president. A carpenter, Focha built this IDES chapel in 1889 with a meeting hall next door. The IDES sponsors annual Holy Ghost *festas* (festivals) to celebrate the Pentecost and Queen Isabel of Portugal, who ,according to legend, fed the people when her prayers for food were answered during a famine. The Holy Ghost festival usually includes a procession and a *festa* queen, who is crowned after Mass. Participants return to the hall for a banquet that includes *sopa e carne* (meat soup) and bread. Dancing often follows the banquet. Below, flowers and Holy Ghost crowns adorn the IDES chapel altar for the 2008 *festa*. (Both, author's collection.)

HOLY GHOST QUEEN. This unidentified queen wearing a traditional white dress holds the Holy Ghost crown. The ornately decorated silver crown represents the crown of Queen Isabel. It is topped with a silver ball, representing the universe; a cross; and a dove in flight, representing the Holy Spirit. (UPEC.)

HOLY GHOST PROCESSION. From left to right are Lavern Duarte, Mary Thomas, Queen Marie Xavier, and Melva Mattos participating in a 1933 Holy Ghost procession in San Leandro. The others are unidentified. (SLHPDC #2532.)

RODRIGUES FAMILY. After the 1906 earthquake, Italian American Mary Delucchi moved from San Francisco to Oakland, where she met Frank Silver Rodrigues working in a factory. At right is their wedding photograph on December 12, 1911. Frank's mother Isabel Rodrigues, born in the Azores, owned a grocery at Davis and Dabner Streets. The newlyweds took over its operation and named it the White Front Grocery. It was typical for mom-and-pop stores to serve neighborhoods before the advent of the supermarket. They moved into the back of the store while Isabel lived next door. In the birthday photograph below, taken around 1938, matriarch Isabel cuts the cake, with Frank and Mary on her right, while seven grandchildren, one great-grandchild, and friends look on. The White Front was closed in 1947. (Both, Eleanor Rodrigues Neves.)

HELEN LAWRENCE. At a time when few women held political office, San Leandro's first female politician served on the city council from 1935 until 1948, three of those years (1941–1944) as mayor. At that time, the mayor was elected by the council rather than by popular vote. Her family immigrated to San Leandro from the Azores when she was a child, and she spoke Portuguese, English, and Spanish. While she was a council member and mayor, Lawrence saw the dedication of Memorial Park and the construction of a new city hall. She also served as the president of the East Bay division of the League of California Cities. She was proud of the "three boys" she launched into public careers: fire chief Manuel Rodriguez, police officer John Cannizzaro, and Mayor Jack Maltester. (Both, Library of Congress.)

OLIVEIRA DAIRY, 1942. Works Progress Administration photographer Russell Lee captioned this photograph with a quote from John Oliveira: "Our favorite stories when I was a child were those which my father and mother told us about their homeland of Portugal. My wife and I have had a good life in the U.S., and we are proud to see our son an honored man of the community. All of us, we are as American as fried chicken now." Oliveira milked about 70 cows daily. His son worked for the First National Bank of San Leandro. These photographs capture the end of an era. Within a few years, houses would replace San Leandro's dairies. (Both, Library of Congress.)

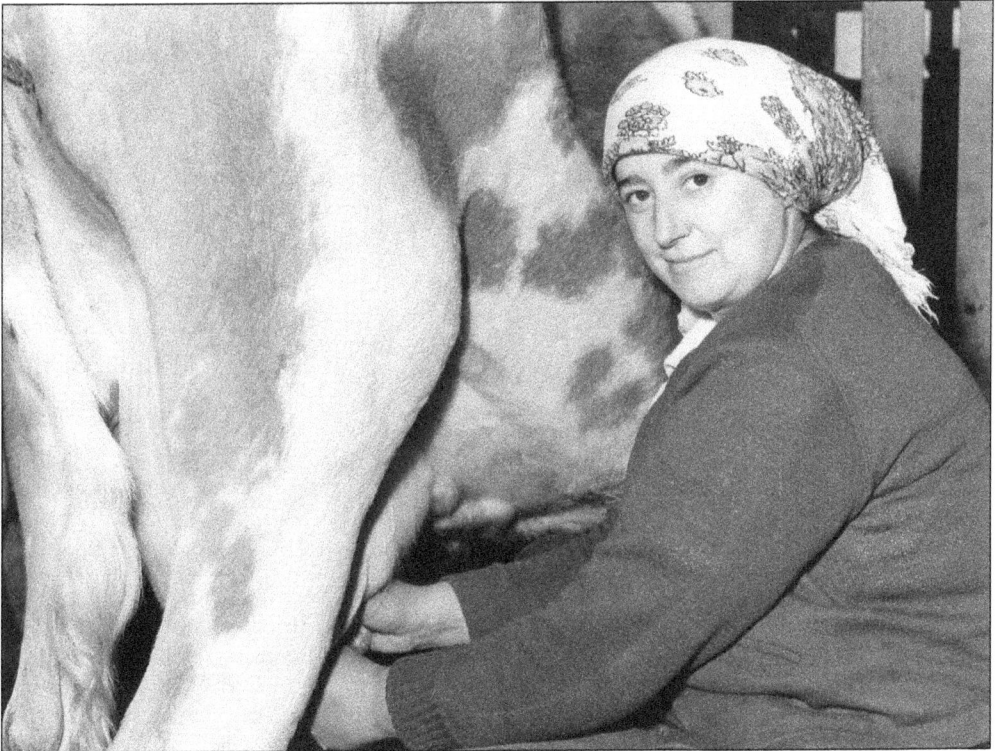

UPEC, 1955. The Oakland UPEC Band poses in front of San Leandro's UPEC building on East Fourteenth Street for the 75th annual convention. In 1964, a new building replaced this old one. The new headquarters included a cultural center, a lecture hall, a museum, and the J. A. Freitas Library, the most complete library of Portuguese materials in California. (San Leandro Museum.)

PORTUGUESE MONUMENT, ROOT PARK. UPEC president Lewis Correia (right) and Christine Medeiros and Maria C. Pachao (in costumes) celebrate Portuguese Immigrant Week in 1970. This white marble *Monument to the Portuguese Immigrant*, sculpted by Numidico Bessone in Portugal, was a gift to San Leandro by members of the UPEC. It was dedicated in 1964 to honor the Portuguese people who settled far from home and built new lives in the United States. (UPEC.)

Four

FARM AND FACTORY
CHERRY CITY TO
THE CENTER OF INDUSTRY

San Leandro historian Harry Shaffer titled his book *A Garden Grows in Eden* because of the farmer's paradise provided by San Leandro's good soil, mild climate, access to water, and central Bay Area location. From the Gold Rush until World War II, agriculture was the mainstay of San Leandro's economy.

San Leandro farmers grew potatoes, tomatoes, corn, currants, peas, fava beans, rhubarb, and other crops. There were many dairies and chicken ranches. Not long after the Lewellings established a fruit tree nursery in the Oakland Fruitvale area, San Leandro farmers developed extensive cherry, apricot, pear, plum, and peach orchards. Newspaper articles boasted of cherries three inches in circumference and three-pound pears.

Agricultural festivals were a means of promotion and marketing, and San Leandro put itself on the map as the Cherry City with its first cherry festival in 1909. In an article for the booklet *Saga of San Leandro*, Bruce Elerick reminisced about this time: "The most spectacular sight of all was the cherry trees in blossom, thousands of cherry trees as far as the eye could see."

Railroads that allowed farmers to get crops to state and national markets also allowed shipment of industrial products. Factories were established in San Leandro in the 1860s. At first, these factories mostly produced agricultural equipment such as tractors. By the 1950s, San Leandro industries still produced tractors but also produced automobiles, calculators, packaging materials, and a host of other products. Outlying farm fields offered cheap land, which city leaders annexed to encourage industrial development and to increase tax revenues despite an extremely low tax rate. As farmland disappeared, boosters began to identify San Leandro as the "City of Industry and Commerce."

In the later decades of the 20th century, San Leandro's heavy industry plants closed. Tractor and truck factories were replaced with retail and service businesses. Light industry, such as North Face, Ghirardelli Chocolate, Otis Spunkmeyer, and Aidells Sausage, still thrives in San Leandro. All take advantage of San Leandro's skilled labor pool and excellent location, with a nearby international airport, major shipping harbor, and truck transportation.

JOHN HENRY BEGIER. An unidentified boy sits on Begier crates. "Cherry King" John Henry Begier, born in Germany, arrived in San Leandro in 1886. A successful farmer with a flair for marketing, he used a wheelbarrow to transport crates of cherries from his orchard to the depot, making him the first to ship across the country. His wheelbarrow became enshrined in San Leandro legend and was often featured in parades. (SLHPDC #2425.)

INDEPENDENCE DAY FLOAT, 1892. John Henry Begier, standing in the middle with arms akimbo, poses with friends and family in front of his cherry-and-produce-decorated float. Begier led his float in this parade while pushing the wheelbarrow he had used to deliver cherries to the depot. (SLHPDC #125.)

LUSCIOUS CHERRIES FOR FREE.
This newspaper insert invited
everyone to San Leandro's first
cherry festival. A bumper crop
of cherries was expected in 1909,
so the Board of Trade decided
to promote San Leandro with
a grand festival. About 25,000
people attended, enjoying a parade,
midway, concessions, concerts,
a baseball game, footraces,
motorcycle races, and a grand ball.
Bessie Best won the title of Cherry
Queen. (City of San Leandro.)

The Citizens of San Leandro cordially
invite the general public to be their
guests on this happy day and participate
in the festivities of this gala occasion

LUSCIOUS CHERRIES FREE

SUPPLEMENT TO THE

Oakland Tribune

JUNE 5TH 1909

FESTIVAL, 1910. After the success
of the first festival, San Leandro's
business community decided to
host a second. Mabel Furtado,
shown posing on the steps with
attendants Myrtle Oakes (left)
and Alzina Demont (right), was
declared the Cherry Festival Queen
after a ballot-box-stuffing scandal.
Attendance was estimated at
45,000. (SLHPDC #1892.)

FESTIVAL, 1911. Festival queen Mabel Cormac and king Alonzo Peralta ride in the royal carriage, leading the longest parade ever, according to *San Leandro Cherry Festivals of the Past*. The 75,000 people attending watched marching bands, decorated automobiles and carriages, service club floats, drill teams, fire wagons, costumed children, and politicians parade through the streets of San Leandro. (SLHPDC #1501.)

FESTIVAL, 1912. Queen Blanche Deutsch rides in style in a car driven by Manuel Garcia. General director Budd Eber is on the horse. Sen. Edward Keating Strobridge officiated at the queen's coronation. Attendance dropped to 40,000, and it was the last full-scale cherry festival for a decade. The parade included the Yerba Buena Navy Band, Frank Gonsalves's German Band, the San Leandro Brass Band, and the Chinese Boys Band. (UPEC.)

PANAMA-PACIFIC EXPOSITION, 1915. Anton Vagar (right) helped create this cherry-covered parade car. San Leandro took the opportunity to show off the town with fruit-and-vegetable-decorated vehicles in the Alameda County Day Parade of the Panama-Pacific Exposition in San Francisco. San Leandro took away many parade prizes, including decorated-automobile first prize for Vagar's cherry-covered car. (SLHPDC #496.)

A SAN LEANDRO CHERRY ORCHARD IN BLOOM
ALAMEDA CO., CALIFORNIA.

CHERRY ORCHARD. This beautiful 1915 postcard touts Cherry City living. The back of the postcard describes the easy transportation to Oakland and San Francisco, and the town: "Population 4,500. Two transcontinental railroads. Five churches. Three schools. Public library. One active women's club whose object is civic and social betterment. . . . Principal products cherries, apricots, berries, rhubarb, peas, tomatoes and corn. Beautiful drive through orchards." (San Leandro Museum.)

FESTIVALS IN THE 1920S. The American Legion Post No. 117 and the ladies auxiliary revived the cherry festival in 1922. These groups were major sponsors for festivals throughout the 1920s. Above, the 1925 queen and her three attendants pose for a photograph. On the far right is Isabel Simas. Below, a view looking west along Estudillo Avenue shows a 1920s festival midway. Note the Ferris wheel carrying riders almost higher than the Herrscher building cupola, the California Market in the old Masonic Building, and the spire of St. Leander's in the distance. (Above, Shirley Vierra Scanlon; below, SLHPDC #163.)

Festival, 1927. Queen Leona Freitas inspects cherries in the tree. This year, the event took place at La Chateauhurst, a new subdivision on East Fourteenth Street near today's city hall. Perhaps more important than the cherries, beginning to be viewed as San Leandro's past, were the free tours that showed off new homes in expanding San Leandro. (San Leandro Museum.)

FESTIVALS IN THE 1930S. Costumed members of the Club Iberico pose in front of their parade float. Complaints about the noise and crowds intruding on the privacy of homeowners led to a new venue at Junction City (East Fourteenth Street and Hesperian Boulevard) in 1931. The Great Depression brought a stop to the celebrations. There was no festival in 1932, and there would not be another full-scale festival until 1972. (SLHPDC #420.)

VIERRA FARM. At Left, Shirley Vierra stands under a cherry tree on the Vierra farm. Below, (from left to right) Joe Simas, a Mrs. Santos, Tony Vierra, Edward Simas, and George Vierra dump the cherries they have picked into crates while Shirley (the child) watches. The five-acre farm was located on Lark Street. The farm also grew tomatoes and corn. Shirley remembers picking cherries when she was 10 years old for 25¢ a bucket, so she could buy a used bicycle. Her daughter now lives in the farmhouse, and Shirley lives next door. (Shirley Vierra Scanlon.)

CHICKEN LANE. Although this photograph shows orchards at the end of Chicken Lane, the street was named for its chicken farms, which were mostly owned by Portuguese settlers. It was renamed Dutton Avenue for Jane Dutton, a single woman who came to the area in 1849, made a fortune running a boarding house in San Francisco, and later had a farm at the end of this street. (SLHPDC #2554.)

BERRY PICKING. Three women and a child stop to pose with their berry harvest from the Mendonça fields around 1920. (SLHPDC #2000.)

PLOWING AND CULTIVATING. Both these photographs were taken in the area that is now the Mulford Gardens subdivision. Above, an unidentified man cultivates his fields with a four-horse team and a disc harrow. Below, George Mendonça plows under the shade of a canopy on a gasoline, three-wheeled Bull Tractor in 1937. (Above, SLHPDC #929; below, SLHPDC #16.)

RHUBARB. In the early decades of the 20th century, many parade floats were designed to show off San Leandro farm products. A truck (above) is decorated with rhubarb, possibly for the Panama-Pacific Exposition, and (below) two men and a woman harvest rhubarb on an unidentified farm. San Leandro farms shipped 14,000 boxes of rhubarb to eastern markets in 1901. No doubt some of the local produce also went to make patent medicine at the California Rhubarb Remedies Company, located on Davis Street. (Above, SLHPDC #2419; below, SLHPDC #2008.)

CUCUMBERS. Fred Supriano, Joseph Supriano, Rocha Mariano, and Leite Mariano pick cucumbers *c.* 1920. The cucumbers might have been sent for processing at the Ravekes Pickle Works. Townspeople would bring pails and kettles to take home their choice of pickles from Ravekes. (SLHPDC #1990.)

HARVESTING AT MENDONÇA FARM. Born in the Azores in 1847, immigrant Joseph Bernardo Mendonça first found work as the foreman at Mulford's farm. Later he acquired his own property and farmed several hundred acres. He was an active member of the UPEC, a director of the Bank of San Leandro, and a Union School trustee. His sons George and Arthur are among the harvesters in this photograph. (SLHPDC #6.)

64

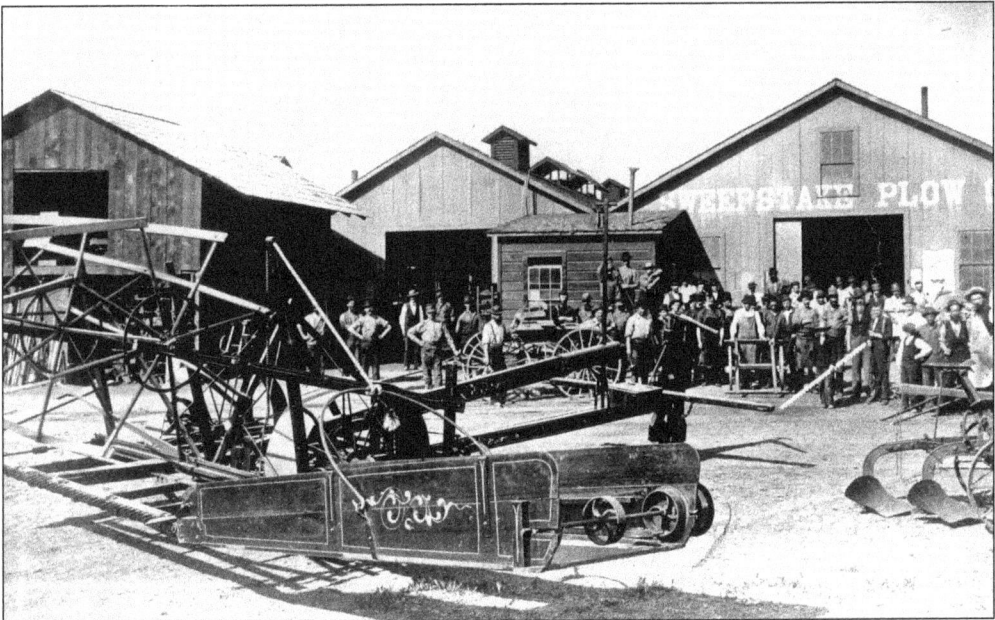

FIRST FACTORIES. Sweepstake Plow, formerly Baker and Hamilton, was San Leandro's first large industry and employed as many as 50 men. It was unable to sustain year-round employment and relocated in 1883. Offsetting this faltering start, a group of local men incorporated as the San Leandro Plow Company and built a foundry, machine shop, wood shop, plow factory, and paint shop on Davis Street. The board of directors included many of San Leandro's business leaders and politicians, including Socrates Huff, T. P. Cary, W. H. Gray, Joseph DeMont, L. C. Morehouse, F. Meyers, and I. H. Bradshaw. (Above, SLHPDC #184; below, SLHPDC #11.)

JUNIOR MONARCH HAY PRESS. Five revolutions of the horses compacted five charges of loose hay in the vertical wooden "dump off" hay press, shown here, to form a bale tied with five wires. Inventor Jacob Price moved his hay press production from Petaluma to San Leandro about 1870. The Toffelmiers later acquired the company and continued to improve and manufacture hay presses until about 1939. (Don Wood.)

HUDSON LUMBER COMPANY, 1912. These mighty cedar logs became cedar slats used in pencil manufacturing. Hudson manufactured pencil slats for almost 90 years, beginning operation in 1909. The company ceased operation in 1998 when it could no longer compete with cheaper imports. It was located at San Leandro Boulevard and Hudson Lane. (SLHPDC #288.)

DANIEL BEST AGRICULTURAL WORKS, 1904. Pioneer and inventor Daniel Best, born in Ohio, came to the Pacific Northwest by wagon train. He moved to San Leandro and bought the San Leandro Plow Company in 1886. The Daniel Best Agricultural Works began manufacturing his newest invention, which combined a grain cleaner with threshers and separators. (SLHPDC #1534.)

DANIEL BEST AGRICULTURAL WORKS. This bucolic view of the factory and town is an engraving from an 1891 *Best Catalogue.* Look for the Best steam combined harvester, a horse-drawn harvester, and a 50-horsepower steam traction engine. The town of San Leandro and the spire of St. Leander's are faintly visible in the upper left background. (SLHPDC #1484.)

BEST STEAM TRACTION ENGINE. After buying Pacific coast manufacturing rights to the Remington steam traction engine in 1888, Best combined the traction engine with a harvester and thresher. The traction engine was much faster than teams of draft animals and pulled the combine over rougher terrain. (SLHPDC #1609.)

BEST MANUFACTURING WORKERS, 1895. Daniel Best (with a beard, seated on a chair in the center front) poses with his employees at the plant. As many as 85 men worked to produce tractors, combines, and machines that were shipped all over the world. (SLHPDC #224.)

TUG-OF-WAR. The *San Leandro Reporter*, on July 4, 1896, noted, "Daniel Best treated his employees to a novel exhibition. The new gasoline traction engine was hitched with large chains to the steam traction engine and both engineers put on full heads of steam. The result was that the gasoline engine hauled the steam engine around the block." This drawing is by Best descendant Quince Galloway. (SLHPDC #1597.)

INTERIOR OF BEST MANUFACTURING, 1904. By the turn of the 20th century, Best had 30 patents to his name. He continued to come up with and patent new ideas, churning out agricultural equipment until he "retired" and sold the company to Holt of Stockton in 1908. At age 70, he then took up other enterprises in San Leandro, including a bank and theater. (SLHPDC #1535.)

C. L. Best Tractor Company. After the sale to Holt, Daniel Best's son C. L. (Leo) Best remained as the manager. The plant continued under the Best name. In 1910, Leo left to start his own C. L. Best Gas Traction Company in Elmhurst. When Holt closed the San Leandro factory in 1913, business leaders were concerned about the loss of a major industry and subscribed $20,000 for C. L. to purchase the old site and return to San Leandro. In 1904, Holt invented a pair of tracks to replace rear-drive wheels for better traction and made the new crawler tractor at his Stockton plant. Best made improvements and began producing a similar crawler tractor in 1913; an early model is pictured below. The two rivals, Holt and Best, merged in 1925 as the Caterpillar Tractor Company. (Above, SLHPDC #851; below, SLHPDC #1530.)

CATERPILLAR TRACTOR COMPANY. A Southern Pacific train leaves the Caterpillar plant with a shipment of tractors around 1935. There were plants in Peoria and San Leandro at this point, and C. L. Best, the first chairman of the board, served until his death in 1951. After World War II, Caterpillar expanded and developed as a multinational corporation. (SLHPDC #589.)

CATERPILLAR. Caterpillar announced the closure of several manufacturing facilities in 1983, including the San Leandro plant. "In closing, Caterpillar broke hearts," said a *Daily Review* article. The buildings have been razed, but the Caterpillar "arch" (surrounding the doors under the Caterpillar sign) was saved and still stands in a slightly different location on Davis Street. (San Leandro Museum.)

DEL MONTE CANNERY. The establishment of a San Leandro cannery in 1899 provided a local market for farmers, easing the constant problem of spoilage before produce could be sold. Located near where the San Leandro Bay Area Rapid Transit (BART) station is today, the California Packing Company later adopted the name of its most famous label, Del Monte. With a canning capacity of 50,000 cases a year, the plant preserved and shipped pears, peaches, apricots, tomatoes, and other fruits and vegetables. The cannery needed many seasonal laborers, hiring as many as 1,000 a year to augment its 70 permanent employees. The cottages visible in this photograph, behind the water tower, housed seasonal workers. The cannery also employed many women and girls. A dried fruit division and an agricultural research division were part of the Del Monte operations. Disappearing farmland and rising land values brought about the closure of the plant in 1973. Also visible in this photograph is the San Leandro Ballpark. (Jim Layton and the San Leandro History Museum.)

72

CANNERY SUPERVISOR. James Edward O'Brien worked for 45 years in the cannery. His first experience at San Leandro Plant No. 8 was during his school vacation in 1900 when he worked on a roller peach-grader and was paid 5¢ an hour for a 10-hour day six days a week. He later became superintendent of the San Leandro plant in 1922, a position he held for 31 years. (Jackie Hayes.)

CANNERY EMPLOYEES. Cannery employee María Dolores Jimenez Gamaza sits on the steps of a cannery cottage with Manuel (left) and Anthony, two of her children. The cannery provided day care for children and rented housing for temporary workers. A recruiting poster from Hawaiian plantations enticed María's parents to emigrate from Spain, but after four years in the islands, they moved on to San Francisco and then San Leandro. (Joseph Diaz.)

FRIDEN CALCULATING MACHINE COMPANY. Carl Friden, a Swedish-born American mechanical engineer and businessman, founded the Friden Calculating Machine Company in 1934. The company rapidly outgrew its rented space in Oakland and built its own plant in San Leandro. From left to right, Gertrude Perry, Carl M. Friden, and chief of police Joseph Peralta pose for the ground-breaking ceremony on June 2, 1936. (SLHPDC #1193.)

FRIDEN CALCULATORS. Friden began manufacturing a fully automatic calculating machine in this modern, efficient plant on 15 acres in San Leandro. A later million-dollar expansion accommodated increased sales and 1,300 employees. Friden died in 1945, but the company continued. Singer Corporation purchased the company in 1963, continuing to manufacture business machines. (SLHPDC #978.)

LARSEN LUMBER. Danish immigrant Jens Larsen founded Larsen Lumber in 1882 on San Leandro Boulevard, selling coal, hay, feed, and lumber. The fourth generation of the family now operates the business on Washington Avenue, where it moved in 1965 to make way for BART. In this 1930s photograph, "Larson" on the front of the building is a sign painter's misspelling of Larsen. (San Leandro Library.)

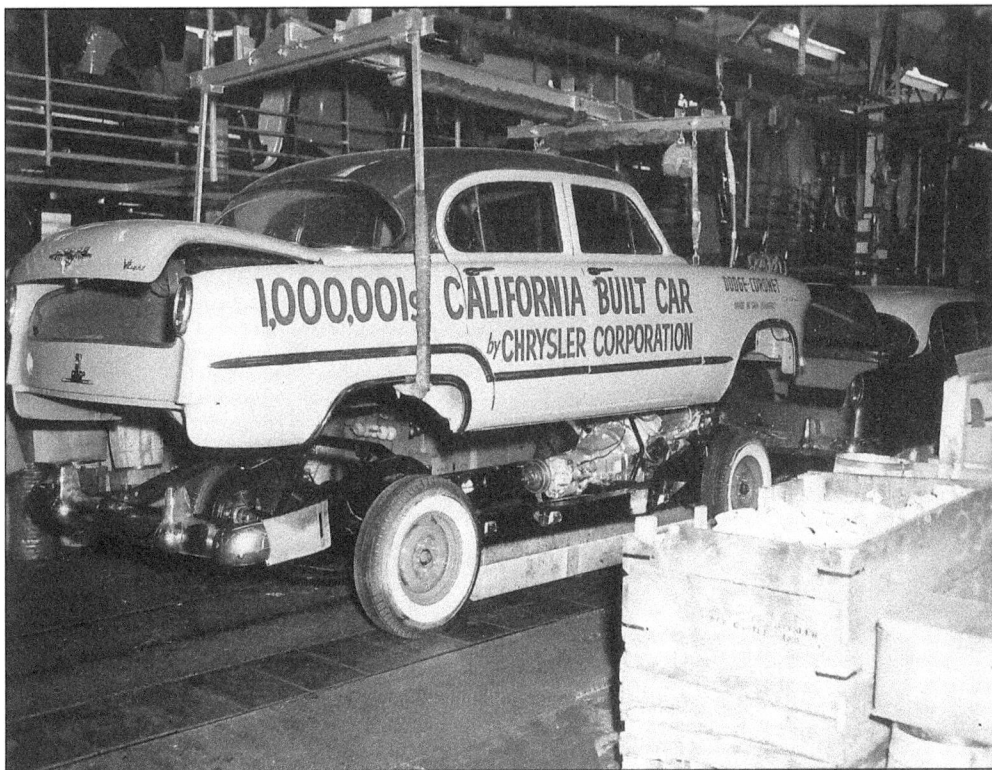

DODGE PLANT. Chrysler began assembling automobiles in its new San Leandro plant in 1948. It was capable of producing automobile bodies at the rate of one every 120 seconds. The company invited everyone to celebrate the 1,000,001st California-built Chrysler car, shown rolling along the assembly line. The doors were opened to the public for tours, and a dinner for invited guests featured Roy Rogers. (San Leandro Museum.)

FARMLAND TO FACTORIES. This aerial image marks four San Leandro industries in 1951. Chrysler had a parts-manufacturing plant as well as the automobile factory. Republic Supply manufactured marine, mill, and oil well materials. Pioneer-Flintkote produced building materials, and Crown Zellerbach manufactured food packaging. These plants were all west of today's Interstate 880 in an area of greenhouses, farm fields, and housing that was increasingly industrialized. (SLHPDC #761.)

BAYFAIR MALL. Macy's, the anchor store for Bayfair Mall, opened to fanfare and a ribbon-cutting ceremony on August 7, 1957. The two-level shopping mall was at the forefront of the retail and service businesses that would replace manufacturing as the most important sector of the San Leandro economy by the end of the 20th century. (Lois Over and the San Leandro Museum.)

Five

VILLAGE TO TOWN
1900 TO 1940

In 1900, there were 2,253 people living in San Leandro. New technologies, a new century, and a growing population brought a sense of community and heightened possibility. Within the first decade of the 20th century, San Leandro had a new library, a new school, a new railroad, and a new cherry festival tradition.

Streetlights, electricity, indoor plumbing, and telephones became commonplace. San Leandro entrepreneur Daniel Best built a car in 1899, starting a rock rolling that by mid-century would be an avalanche of roads, freeways, and parking lots for the ubiquitous automobile. Baseball, parades, dozens of social and service organizations, and the new "talkies" at the theaters provided entertainment.

More than 400 young men in San Leandro registered for the draft, and many saw service during World War I. Townspeople responded generously to an active Red Cross organization and Liberty Bond sales. C. L. Best introduced the Best Tank and geared up production for the war.

The Great Depression hit San Leandro with layoffs and hard times, although many were still farmers and could put food on the table. Works Projects Administration funds provided a new city hall and a new sewer system, as well as other improvements around town.

Although still a farm town, San Leandro began to take on the character of a suburb in these decades. Oakland and San Francisco were now densely populated cities, so real estate developers advertised the quiet garden living of single-family homes with quick and easy transportation to city centers to attract new San Leandro residents.

The town continued to increase in population and area. By 1940, there were 14,601 people living in San Leandro.

Horseless Carriage. Driver C. L. Best shows off the automobile, possibly the first in Alameda County, that he and his father built in 1899. Daniel Best described it as "a work of art . . . solid rubber tires . . . and with all the grace of a mud scow." The seven-horse-power, vapor-electric water-cooled "gasoline engine of two opposed cylinders" could attain a top speed of 20 miles per hour. (SLHPDC #1485.)

Parade. Children parade down Haywards Road along the Plaza, celebrating the Alameda County Fair in August 1905 or 1906. They are passing H. F. Eber's Grove Market, F. S. Dickinson's Drug Store, the Odd Fellows Hall with C.H. Gray's Grocery, Hardware and Post Office, and F. Meyers's General Store, Silva's Oyster and Chop House, Christensen's San Leandro Hotel (with people standing on its balcony), and O. J. Lynch's drugstore. (SLHPDC #664.)

BRIDGES. The first bridge over San Leandro Creek at today's East Fourteenth Street was built in 1854. The covered bridge shown here was built in 1876. According to Bessie Best, "it rattled. Oh, it was terrible! Made so much noise when you went through it." Left of the bridge is the trestle used by the Oakland, San Leandro, and Haywards Electric Railway. In 1901, a concrete bridge replaced the old wooden bridge. It is shown in this 1916 photograph below as a streetcar passes over it. (Above, SLHPDC #804; below, SLHPDC #738.)

THE CANNON AND HERRSCHER BUILDINGS, 1908. The plaza cannon, known as "Little Betsy," was a gift from the navy and had been captured during the Spanish-American War. It was later moved to Root Park and then fell victim to a scrap-iron drive for World War II. Bavarian-born Joseph Herrscher arrived in San Leandro in 1882. He built two distinctive buildings on the Plaza in the 1890s (look for the buildings with cupolas). He and his wife, Clara, also operated a store on a corner opposite the Herrscher buildings. Herrscher was involved in the organization of the cannery and the First Hebrew Congregation, and he donated the lot for the Little Shul. Below, Mr. and Mrs. Herrscher pose outside the Herrscher Cheap Cash Store. (Above, SLHPDC #415; below, SLHPDC #62.)

JUNCTION HOUSE. The Junction House stood at the intersection of Hesperian Boulevard and East Fourteenth Street in an area known as Junction City. Tom Lavin is driving the carriage; Jack Lavin is seated on the far right. This photograph was taken around 1900. (SLHPDC #203.)

BEACH OUTING, 1910. Young men and women enjoy the fresh air and sunshine at the white sand beach that used to be at the foot of Davis Street. (SLHPDC #1378.)

BASEBALL. Above, a large crowd watches a baseball game in the San Leandro Baseball Club stadium at Parrott Street and San Leandro Boulevard. The stadium, built in 1909, could seat 400 people. Below, the Best Tractors team takes the Mission League championship in 1918. San Leandro's powerhouse Tractors and Cruisers teams sent several players to the big leagues, including Walter "Sea Cap" Christensen, Lew Fonseca, Taylor Douthit, Richard "Rowdy Dick" Bartell, and Ralph "Red" Kress. (Above, SLHPDC #615; below, SLHPDC #481.)

MARY BROWN AND THE SAN LEANDRO LIBRARY. The newspaper office, O. J. Lynch's drugstore, and an oyster company office were repositories over the years for books shared by the San Leandro Library Association, formed in 1872. Finally, the board of trustees decided to fund a free public library. The first librarian, Mary Brown, opened the new library in rooms at the city hall in 1906. When refugees from the 1906 earthquake needed space in the city hall, the library moved to the Gorman Building. In 1909, with funds from philanthropist Andrew Carnegie, the library got its own building at the site of today's main library. Brown was the librarian until she retired in 1938. This building was demolished in 1959, but look for the Carnegie library lampposts and gold "Public Library" letters at today's main library. (Right, San Leandro Museum; below, SLHPDC #1330.)

LINCOLN SCHOOL. By the 1900s, the Union School was crowded with a growing population of San Leandro children. A new building, called the Lincoln School, was built in 1910, and the old building was demolished. In the photograph below, a Lincoln School class poses for a photograph in 1911. For half a century, elementary school students learned their lessons at this imposing building on West Joaquin. In 1966, the elementary students were moved out, and the building housed the continuation high school and the school district offices. Then the building was sold to a developer and razed in 1978. The Lincoln School bell was saved and is now at the San Leandro Main Library. (Above, San Leandro Museum; below, SLHPDC #1926.)

SOUTHERN PACIFIC DEPOT. San Leandro's farmers and manufacturers shipped many products from this depot, built in 1898. Passengers used the depot as well until World War II. It was sold to the San Leandro Historical Railway Society in 1988 and was moved a short distance to Thrasher Park, where it now houses a railway museum and HO model railroad display. (Author's collection.)

WESTERN PACIFIC DEPOT. The town celebrated the new rail line connecting the East Bay area to San Francisco and the opening of the Western Pacific Railroad Depot on Martinez Street at Davis Street. Businesses closed, and about 2,000 people gathered to see the first train arrive at the San Leandro station on August 22, 1910. The steamer *Telephone* linked the Oakland pier and San Francisco. (SLHPDC #2049.)

MOTORIZED FIRE EQUIPMENT. Henry Bormann, Bert Rodgers, town marshal Joseph Peralta, driver Chris Hopper, and fire chief Budd Eber pose with San Leandro's first motorized truck, a 1913 Seagrave chemical hose wagon (right). Although he resigned after town trustees slashed his request for equipment funds, Chief Eber was re-elected and remained as the fire chief until he retired in 1919. (Ray Jannson.)

ST. JOSEPH'S HALL. "Joe Burnett won a pie-eating contest at the . . . show held at St. Joseph's Hall," noted the *Reporter* in 1889. Built in 1869, Smith's Hall was bought by St. Leander's in 1884 and was renamed St. Joseph's. San Leandrans gathered here for meetings, programs, and graduations, and it was the home of the San Leandro Boys' Club before it was razed in 1961. (SLHPDC #1976.)

BEST BUILDING AND THEATRE. After Daniel Best retired from manufacturing, he decided to build a business block downtown. The Best Building at the corner of East Fourteenth Street and Estudillo Avenue was constructed in 1910 and was opened for business as the San Leandro Bank in 1911. It is the only early-20th-century plaza building still appearing much as it did when it was completed. Best built the theater shown in the photograph below around 1912, next door to the Best Building. From left to right are Lloyd Bridges Sr. (father of the actor), Frank Halliday, Paul Simpson, Van Blix, and ? Dooley (the movie operator). Lloyd Bridges Jr., the star of many adventure films and the television series *Sea Hunt*, was born in San Leandro in 1913. (Above, SLHPDC #754; below, SLHPDC #173.)

MASONIC TEMPLE. The Masonic Temple Building, still standing proudly at the corner of East Fourteenth Street and West Joaquin Avenue, was dedicated on April 15, 1910. It is the home of Eden Lodge No. 113 of the Freemasons. The Eden Lodge was the first fraternal order in San Leandro, when it was established in 1857. The first floor has had various tenants, including the Hirschman Creamery and Candy Store, shown below. (Above, SLHPDC #344; below, SLHPDC #622.)

ALAMEDA COUNTY INFIRMARY. This hospital and farm provided care for the ill who could not afford a doctor's visit and for the elderly without family to care for them. The first patient was admitted in 1864. This photograph, taken around 1900, shows a man carrying meals to the patients. (San Leandro Museum.)

FAIRMONT HOSPITAL. Complaints about the county infirmary, with its crowded, aging buildings too near fly-infested barnyards, led to renovations and a new name, the Fairmont Hospital, in 1919. This photograph, taken around 1940, shows many new buildings as well as the old Foothill Boulevard before the freeway. (San Leandro Museum.)

ESTUDILLO AVENUE. A 1920s automobile excursion is ready to roll on Estudillo. Only a few decades earlier, Bessie Best remembered when her family would walk a "mile and a half up the Estudillo Avenue . . . into the hills . . . And we'd go . . . sucker-hole swimming. . . . We'd run into a lot of cattle, and they'd chase you and boy we'd run just like we'd been shot out of a gun." (SLHPDC #372.)

AUTOMOBILES. Joseph Correa (driver, first car on the left) and his brother John (the passenger) line up their car with other automobiles around 1915 in front of the Estudillo House. Joseph was the first mail carrier in San Lorenzo. Their father, Frank Correa, grew currants on a farm off Hesperian Boulevard. (Bernice Correa Thomas.)

ESTUDILLO HOUSE PICNIC GROUNDS. The Estudillo House was used frequently for San Leandro celebrations. Here, the town's citizens gather under the picnic grounds grape arbor to honor World War I veterans. After 74 years as the town's premier hotel and restaurant, the Estudillo House was razed in 1929. (SLHPDC #499.)

JOSEPH F. PERALTA. Behind the city jail, deputy marshal Louis Bacon (left) and town marshal Joseph Peralta show off an illegal still confiscated in a Prohibition-era raid. Peralta, the great-grandson of Ygnacio Peralta, became the town marshal in 1912 and the chief of police in 1928, where he remained until his retirement in 1945. (SLHPDC #198.)

HERMINIA PERALTA DARGIE (1861–1929) AND THE CASA PERALTA. Granddaughter of Ygnacio and Rafaela Peralta, Herminia grew up with the Spanish customs of her *Californio* ancestors at a time when that past was disappearing. She married William Dargie, publisher of the *Oakland Tribune*. After his death, she traveled extensively in Europe. She returned with a young Spanish engineer, Antonio Martín, to remodel the home on West Estudillo she had acquired from her aunts. His 1926 remodel fused Spanish elements such as arches, tiles, balconies, and a walled garden onto the 1901 home. The front wall displays adobe bricks rescued from the demolition of Antonio Peralta's 1821 Rancho San Antonio home. (Left, SLHPDC #1971; below, author's collection.)

CASA PERALTA DON QUIXOTE TILES. Lovely handmade tiles imported from Toledo, Spain, were used for fountains and decorative elements throughout the grounds and to frame interior fireplaces. The tiles along the courtyard wall tell the story of Don Quixote, Miguel de Cervantes's famous would-be knight who tried to right all wrongs in 17th-century Spain. Above, a close-up of a tile depicts Don Quixote. Below, tile contractor Juan Sabido, far left, and two workers pose around the fountain topped by a statue of Sancho Panza, Don Quixote's squire. Martín was reputed to be a perfectionist and exacting taskmaster, making the tile workers tear out and redo the fountain four times before he was satisfied. (Above, SLHPDC #1478; below, Carmen Avelar.)

CHUMALIA STREET. Frank Barradas, Frank Leslie, Oscar Burnett, George Wagner, Frankie Aber, and an unidentified driver pose in a Buick Autocar at 115 Chumalia in the early 1900s. At left, about 30 years later, Eleanor O'Brien (left) and Frankie Aber (right) pose with child Jackie O'Brien. Chumalia was named for Jesus María Estudillo, whose baby pronunciation of his name resulted in the sound "Chumalia." (Both, Jackie Hayes.)

ALTA MIRA CLUB. The Alta Mira Club was formed in 1907 and was the first California Federated Women's Club in San Leandro. Alta Mira bought the 1860 Peralta house on Lafayette Avenue in 1926 when it was slated for destruction and preserved the beautiful home in its original splendor. This 1920 photograph (above) of the Alta Mira choral group was taken at an unidentified home on East Fourteenth Street. (SLHPDC # 588.)

DAHLIAS. Dr. Luther Michael (right) presents dahlias to Gov. C. C. Young, c. 1929. When he was not tending San Leandro's sick, Dr. Michael tended his spectacular dahlias. He organized the San Leandro Dahlia Society in 1925, as well as flower shows that attracted as many as 40,000 people. Dahlias were named the official San Leandro flower in 1927, and the Dahlia Society still holds well-attended flower shows. (SLHPDC #2321.)

THRASHER PARK SWIM TANK. Beatrice Rodrigues (look for the handwritten nickname "Pee Wee" to find her) and friends clear the pool for a group photograph, c. 1930. Thrasher Park is the oldest park in the city. The swim tank is gone, but today people enjoy the softball field, skateboard park, picnic areas, and the San Leandro Historical Railway Society museum. (Eleanor Rodrigues Neves.)

FARRELLY POOL. Swimmers c. 1938 pose in front of the Farrelly Pool, which was built with funds provided in the estate of Henrietta Farrelly. Located on Dutton Avenue adjacent to the Roosevelt School, the pool still provides fun and exercise for swimmers today. (SLHPDC #897.)

SCHOOL BANDS. Charles Way, director of instrumental music in San Leandro schools from about 1911 until 1954, directs the San Leandro all-schools band in this 1928 photograph. Henrietta Farrelly donated funds for his salary as well as music and equipment for a band. (SLHPDC #2110.)

MCKINLEY SCHOOL. San Leandro's population increased by more than 2,000 people in the 1910s, and it was necessary to add two more schools soon after the Lincoln School was completed. The Washington and McKinley Schools were dedicated in 1917. This photograph shows a 1930s McKinley safety patrol. (San Leandro Museum.)

BROADMOOR. Developers Breed and Bancroft opened the first Broadmoor tract in 1908. The New Broadmoor subdivision advertised San Leandro as "the Garden Section of the East Bay." It was, according to the sales pamphlet, "the only remaining section of one of San Leandro's famous old orchards." The beautiful neighborhood has preserved many of its old homes. (SLHPDC #1901.)

BROADMOOR PRESCHOOL. The 1939–1940 class of the Broadmoor Preschool poses for the camera. The federal government's Work Projects Administration provided funds to launch the school, which opened in 1939. The Broadmoor Preschool still operates as a parent cooperative nursery school. (Marcia Cronin.)

OLD HIGH SCHOOL. High school students had to leave town for school until the 1920s. This school was built on Bancroft Avenue in 1926 as a junior and senior high by the consolidated Oakland–San Leandro district. It was razed in 1953, much to the dismay of many San Leandrans. The new Bancroft Junior High School opened in 1954 on the old high school site. (San Leandro Museum.)

NEW SAN LEANDRO HIGH. This 1950 aerial photograph shows the second San Leandro High School in the midst of new housing. It was constructed in 1948 on Bancroft Avenue about a mile south of the old school site. San Leandro withdrew from the Oakland consolidated district and formed its own San Leandro Unified School District in 1952. (SLHPDC #26.)

VETERAN'S MEMORIAL BUILDING. Dedicated in 1934, the Veteran's Memorial Building on Bancroft Avenue was erected in memory of those veterans who had lost their lives in service. It housed the activities of the San Leandro Post No. 117, American Legion, Veterans of Foreign Affairs, and the Spanish War Veterans. During World War II, it housed Battery B of the 344th Anti-Aircraft Artillery Search Light Battalion. (SLHPDC #1204.)

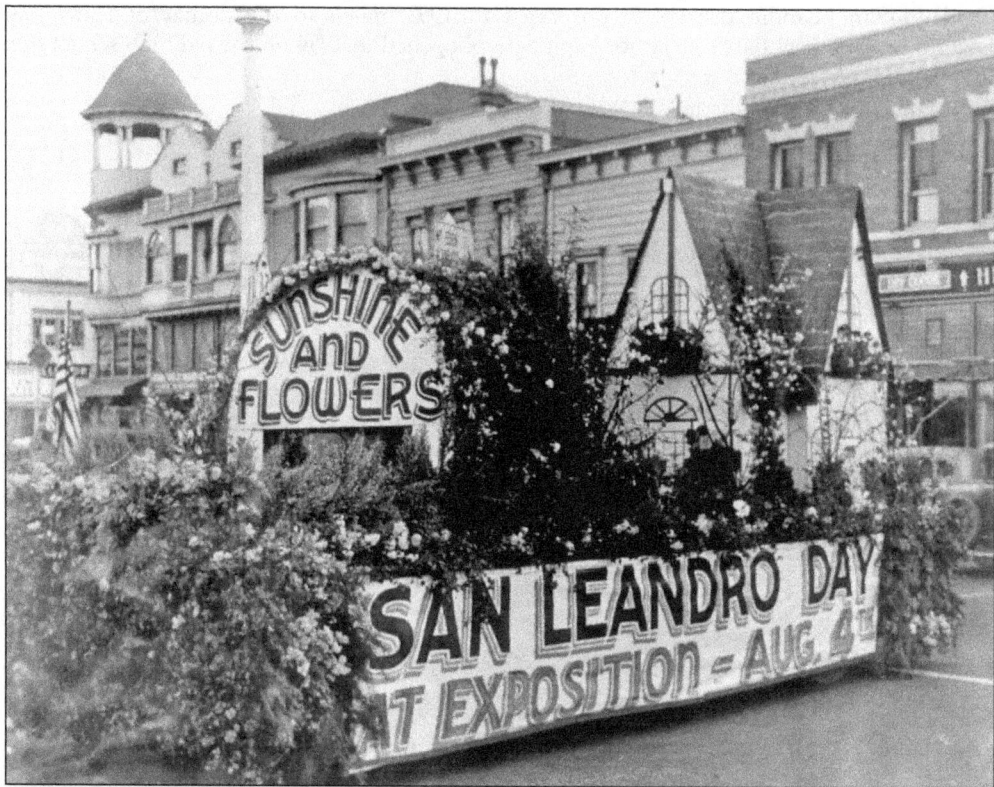

CITY OF SUNSHINE AND FLOWERS, 1939. Either on its way to the Golden Gate International Exposition or just for advertising, a chamber of commerce float motors along Washington Avenue. In between billing itself as the "Cherry City" and the "City of Industry," San Leandro was advertised as the "City of Sunshine and Flowers" because of its many flower nurseries (notably orchid, gardenia, and rose greenhouses) and nationally known dahlias. (SLHPDC #862.)

GOLDEN GATE INTERNATIONAL EXPOSITION, 1939. These high school girls are on field trip to the exposition on Treasure Island. Dozens of baskets filled with 6,000 flowers grown in San Leandro were emptied on Treasure Island for San Leandro Day at the fair. (SLHPDC #876.)

FERRY. The Key System added special runs and a cocktail lounge to the auto-passenger ferry called the *San Leandro* during the Golden Gate Exposition. Built in 1923, it had a steel hull, and a diesel turbo-electric engine powering screw propellers. The *San Leandro* was one of a fleet of ferries used to complete travel between East Bay rail lines and San Francisco. (San Leandro Museum.)

CAMPAIGN HEADQUARTERS. Campaigners pose in front of the 1936 election headquarters for Franklin D. Roosevelt, his vice-presidential candidate John Nance Garner, and congressional candidate John H. Tolan. There were 2,389 votes for Democrat Roosevelt and 1,853 votes for Republican Hoover in San Leandro. Representative Tolan was re-elected to his sixth term. (SLHPDC #603.)

NEW CITY HALL. Even after leasing four rooms in the UPEC building on East Fourteenth Street, the old town hall on Davis Street was inadequate for the growing population of San Leandro in the 1930s. With a Public Works Administration grant providing almost half the costs, a new city hall was built at 835 East Fourteenth Street. (Lois Over and San Leandro Museum.)

PELTON OFFICE. Allen E. Pelton was the mayor of San Leandro from 1916 until 1924. He also served on the board of trustees and as city manager. He instituted the commission form of government, arranged for Henry Root to donate land for a park, and later had Root Park enlarged with Works Progress Administration labor. A realtor and developer, Pelton's home and office on East Fourteenth Street were famous for its garden. (SLHPDC #265.)

PELTON CENTER. Pelton's son Aylmer developed the open-air shopping Pelton Center in 1948 on the site of the Pelton office and land. It was built to accommodate the increased reliance and popularity of the automobile, with a street bisecting the mall to allow drivers to pass through and reach the parking spaces provided near every storefront. (Lois Over and San Leandro Museum.)

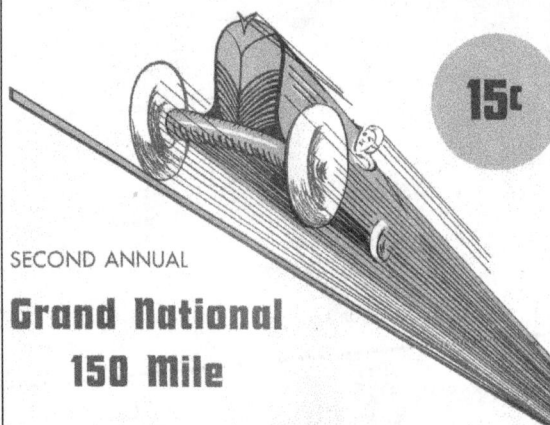

FARM TO RACETRACK TO MALL. John and Annie Coelho, their five children, and brother Thomas Coelho are outside their farmhouse. The Coelhos, from the Azores, settled in San Leandro in 1880 and farmed about 80 acres near today's Hesperian. Their land became the Oakland Speedway (1931–1941), then the Oakland Stadium (1946–1955), and finally Bayfair Mall in 1957. (Coehlo family and *A History of the Oakland Speedway* by Tom Motter.)

OAKLAND SPEEDWAY. This one-mile, banked, oval track in San Leandro brought the thrills of American Automobile Association–sanctioned racing to as many as 20,000 fans on "the fastest dirt track in the country." This program's midget race was one of several types in later years, including big car, stock car, and motorcycle races, some on the half-mile inside track added in 1935. (*A History of the Oakland Speedway* by Tom Motter.)

104

Six

MAJOR METROPOLITAN SUBURB

1940 TO THE PRESENT

World War II transformed California. Shipyards were built almost overnight as the nation quickly mobilized. Federal contracts for military supplies expanded production. Job opportunities brought tens of thousands of new people to the Bay Area. The population explosion continued as people from every state poured into California in the 1950s and 1960s. San Leandro's population almost doubled between 1940 and 1950, from 14,601 to 27,542. It more than doubled in the next decade, reaching 65,962 by 1960. Truck farms that had been supplying vegetables, fruit, and cut flowers to the Bay Area became housing developments supplying people.

The *Wall Street Journal* called San Leandro a "model municipality" in 1966, praising its spending on civic improvement such as the marina and library while keeping taxes and debt extremely low. San Leandro hit the national press with troubling issues as well. A *Newsweek* article on "white flight" used San Leandro as an example, and a U.S. commission on civil rights held hearings on housing discrimination in San Leandro. Realtors and homeowners groups had effectively barred minority families, creating a community that was 99 percent Caucasian in 1960. After California's Rumford Fair Housing Act, those demographics began to change. In the 1980s and 1990s, California's population achieved striking ethnic diversity and so did San Leandro.

Freeways and almost universal automobile ownership increased mobility. Malls and business districts flourished in outlying areas. Decentralized business areas brought a decline in many downtowns, including San Leandro's, and the population increase brought traffic congestion throughout the Bay Area. In the 1960s and 1970s, downtown redevelopment added parking and rerouted traffic. Now the city is working to create an attractive and pedestrian-friendly downtown with specialty businesses, while a newly landscaped history walk on West Estudillo Avenue links downtown to BART.

Today San Leandro has almost filled in its 15 square miles. The 80,000 people who live in San Leandro work at a variety of jobs in a major metropolitan area. San Leandro's greatest resource today is not acorns, or cattle hides, or rich soil, but people—ready to weave their stories into the transformations of the future.

DRAFTEES, JUNE 16, 1941. Although the United States was neutral until after the bombing of Pearl Harbor on December 7, 1941, a draft was instituted with the Selective Training and Service Act of 1940. From Left to right are Robert Johns, Superano Morgado, Manuel Gomes, Robert Whitcomb, Bill Bettencourt, Thomas Rice, Wallace Pells, and Leslie J. Freeman, the chairperson of the local draft board. (SLHPDC #1206.)

FRED KOREMATSU. Posing in the family's nursery, Korematsu (in front) was an American of Japanese ancestry. He was arrested in San Leandro for refusing to report for internment during World War II. His case went to the U.S. Supreme Court, where he lost. His determined battle for justice succeeded in 1983 when a federal court vacated the conviction. In 1998, he was awarded the Presidential Medal of Freedom. (Karen Korematsu.)

106

BATTERY B. The 344th Anti-Aircraft Artillery Search Light Battalion poses on the steps of the Veterans Building, where they were housed during World War II. They manned anti-aircraft guns and searchlights in the East Bay hills. Capt. Whitney Rosaaen is in the center of the first row holding the dog. After the war, Rosaaen joined the San Leandro police force, where he served for 25 years. (Olga Rosaaen.)

WILL STRUT HOSIERY. Nylon was scarce during World War II because of its use for parachutes and other military supplies. When word got out that nylon stockings were available at the Will Strut Hosiery, located at Foothill Boulevard and Miramar Avenue, thousands of people lined up before the doors opened in the hopes of buying stockings. (San Leandro Museum.)

CLASSROOM, 1942. Russell Lee, a Works Progress Administration photographer, took these pictures of a San Leandro classroom in 1942. He captioned the photograph above, "Classroom in a grade school of San Leandro, California. All children with their hands raised are of Portuguese descent, and are proud of it." San Leandro had a majority Portuguese population until the post–World War II population explosion changed Bay Area demographics. In the photograph below, a boy draws on the chalkboard to promote bonds to help the war effort. (Both, Library of Congress.)

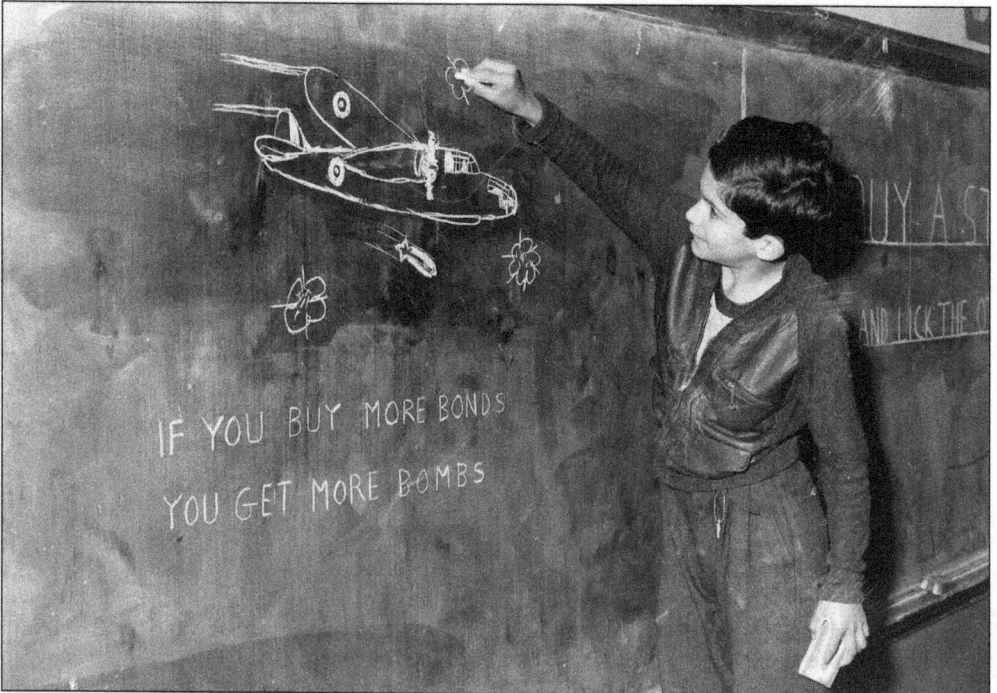

IF YOU BUY MORE BONDS
YOU GET MORE BOMBS

SAN LEANDRO PLAZA, 1945. The streetcar tracks and palm trees are gone, and automobiles dominate the scene in this view of downtown during the war years. (SLHPDC #1973.)

SAN LEANDRO POLICE, 1945. San Leandro's protectors are, from left to right: (first row) Cecile Bretschneider, Calvin Mellor, Sam Davina, Jack Silva, Capt. Art Lamoureux, Chief Joe Peralta, Andres Poulsen, John Cannizzaro, Ray MacCallum, and Alice Tiffin; (second row) Jack Ashman, Steve Lagomarsino, Ambrose Arvini, Ted Werner, Ed Motta, Les DiPaola, Tony Cano, Jack Voluntine, Selo Capitola, and Tony Gomes; (third row) Harry Rose, Bernard O'Neill, Herb Bretschneider, and Fred Haller. (SLHPDC #506.)

OAKLAND STADIUM. In 1946, a racetrack was built on the site of the old Oakland Speedway. The paved, five-eighths-mile track had a tight corner with the highest banked turn in America. A quarter-mile track was added inside. This 1953 aerial shows the racetrack and the fan-shaped Stadium Auto Movie and Oakland Drive-In theaters. (*A History of the Oakland Stadium* by Tom Motter.)

STOCK CAR RACE. Fifteen-thousand fans watch Roger Ward leading Johnny Soares in a 250-lap Western Racing Association race that Andy Linden would win. Soares finished second. The track held midget, big car, roadster, hardtop, and stock car races. (*A History of the Oakland Stadium* by Tom Motter.)

110

TROPHY TIME. Emily Ray presents Marvin Panch with a trophy at the Oakland Stadium. This is probably a fastest-qualifier trophy for the Grand National race on August 1, 1954. Panch went on to greater glory, but 1954 was the end for the track. Construction would soon begin on the new mall, and by 1957, shoppers replaced race cars on the old Coelho farmland. (Emily Ray.)

EAST FOURTEENTH STREET AND THE DEL MAR THEATER. The Del Mar opened in 1941, showing Charlie Chaplin in *The Great Dictator*. It was located on East Fourteenth Street between Dutton and Euclid Avenues. It seated more than 1,100 people. During World War II, the Del Mar provided the kick-off celebration for a bond drive and required the purchase of a war bond for admission. (SLHPDC #1203.)

SUBURBAN LIVING. Children play in their yard on a warm day in this example of the pleasures of suburban life. San Leandro realtors and developers advertised the middle-class ideal of single-family homes in a community with open space, while the city encouraged industrial development to keep homeowner taxes low. (SLHPDC #2045.)

NEW HOMES. The Clark family has recently moved in to their new home on 141st Street in the spring of 1943. There was a desperate need for housing during and after World War II as people poured in from everywhere to find work in Bay Area war industries. The GI Bill's low-interest loans to veterans made it possible for many families to own their homes. (SLHPDC #621.)

LUCKY STORE GRAND OPENING, 1948. City manager L. L. Olson, Merchant's Association president Arthur C. Ames, Councilman Sam Vlahos, and Councilwoman Helen Lawrence are on hand at the special luncheon for opening day of the new supermarket at Juana and East Fourteenth Streets. The spacious and ultra-modern Lucky store was hailed by the *Wall Street Journal* as "ten years ahead of its time" for innovations such as metal shopping carts, store directories, wide aisles, self-service in all departments, and ample parking. It even had a soda fountain. In 1950, Lucky also moved its headquarters to a 66-acre site among San Leandro's truck farms. Below, a postcard advertises the new supermarket. (Above, SLHPDC #848; below, Lois Over.)

HING KEE LAUNDRY. Gee Hen Jung emigrated from China and eventually settled in San Leandro. In 1917, he opened a laundry on Carpentier Street, an area with a small Chinese community, as early as the 1870s. When the building was razed c. 1980, the sign was saved and is now on display at the San Leandro History Museum. (SLHPDC #1323.)

HERRSCHER BUILDING FIRE. San Leandro firefighters battle a spectacular fire at the Herrscher building facing Washington Avenue at West Estudillo Avenue. The fire overwhelmed the 22 men of the San Leandro Fire Department, as well as their 1921 and 1926 Seagrave pumpers and 1927 REO Speed Wagon, and the building was destroyed. (*San Leandro Fire Department History-Yearbook.*)

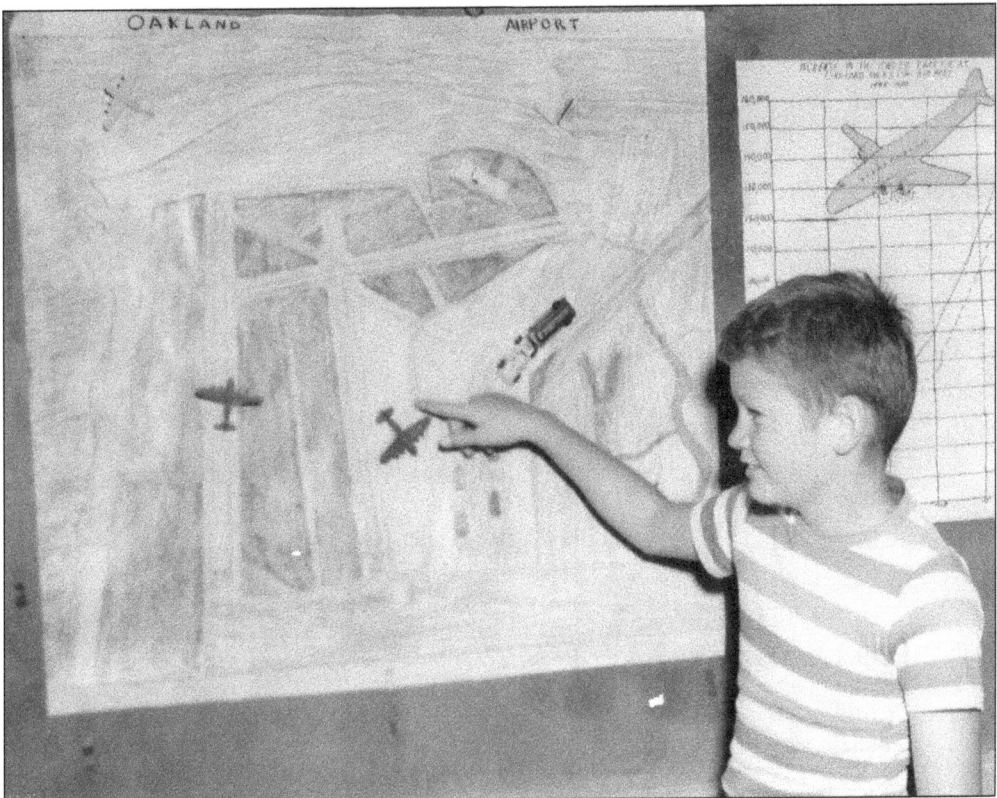

TRANSPORTATION PROJECT. A student c. 1950 in Coleman Herts's class explains a project on the Oakland Airport. After teaching for a few years, Herts was the audio-visual supervisor for San Leandro's schools. The student's graph shows a steep curve of increasing passenger traffic at the airport. As the railroads were earlier, the airport has been an essential element of transportation for San Leandro. (Fran Herts.)

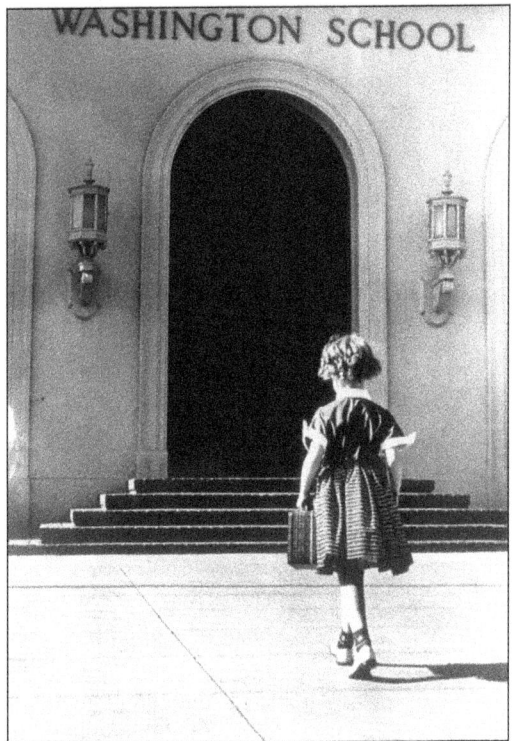

WASHINGTON SCHOOL. An unidentified student carries her lunch box into one of San Leandro's oldest schools in this photograph, taken in approximately 1955. To accommodate new San Leandro families and the baby boom, the San Leandro Unified School District opened several new schools between 1947 and 1965 and then had to close schools as enrollment declined. (SLHPDC #1077.)

BIKES AT THE LIBRARY. Children attending the first movie screened at the San Leandro Library parked their bicycles outside on October 11, 1949. The old building was no longer adequate for the greatly increased population, and in 1959, the old library was torn down to make way for a new, larger facility. (SLHPDC #2555.)

COMMUNITY LIBRARY. San Leandro passed Measure L, a library bond, and built a new library on the site of the old Carnegie building. Dedicated on January 15, 1961, it included two garden courts, a lecture hall, several meeting rooms, and an art gallery, making it truly a community-gathering place. It was more than 44,660 square feet and had a capacity for 120,000 books. (San Leandro Library.)

SAN LEANDRO MARINA. Shoreline development in the late 1950s provided a boat harbor as well as four miles of shoreline walks, bike paths, a golf course, and a 30-acre park, with picnic and play areas, which all created a beautiful place to enjoy bay views and escape the busy city. At right is a closer view of the boat harbor. Look for the building on the left edge and the sign behind it to identify Bill Peluso's Blue Dolphin Restaurant, which opened in 1965. The restaurant closed on January 1, 1996, after more than 30 years of hosting countless conferences, proms, weddings, birthday parties, dinners, dances, and banquets. (Both, San Leandro Museum.)

SAN LEANDRO PLAZA, 1962. San Leandrans gather for the dedication of the new downtown promised by Plaza Project 1. Residential shopping centers such as Bayfair Mall and increasing traffic brought a decline in the downtown business area. Redevelopment projects tried to address the problems by rerouting traffic, adding parking, and providing funds for improvements. (SLHPDC #1078.)

SAN LEANDRO PLAZA, 1960S. This view shows the Plaza after the first redevelopment. Washington Avenue still formed the western side of the plaza triangle, with angled parking along the edge. The second redevelopment project would end Washington as a through street and demolish some of the old buildings to create a much larger parking area. (Lois Over and the San Leandro Museum.)

ART LARSEN. Tennis Hall-of-Fame champion Larsen (left) is 14 years old in this photograph of his first tournament win at San Francisco's Olympic Club. He won the U.S. Open Men's Singles championship in 1950. Nicknamed "Tappy" for his habit of touching things with his tennis racket for good luck, Larsen still lives in San Leandro. A motor scooter accident in 1956 on Davis Street ended his career. (Art Larsen.)

TONY LEMA. San Leandro's Tony Lema Golf Course is named for this professional golfer, here demonstrating his golf swing on the *Ed Sullivan Show.* Lema won the British Open in 1964, as well as 10 tour events, and he was twice a member of the Ryder Cup team. He and his wife, Betty, were killed in an airplane crash in 1966. (Harry Lema.)

NEW SCHOOLS. New schools were needed to accommodate baby-boomer children and new families. Marina High (above) on Wicks Boulevard was in San Leandro but was part of the San Lorenzo Unified School District. Pacific High (below), located on Marina Boulevard, opened in 1960, with a distinctive round main building. Its lit football field was named for school superintendent C. Burrell. Both were closed in the mid-1980s. (Above, *Valhalla* yearbooks; below, *Timaran* yearbook.)

AERIAL, 1963. East Bay urban sprawl is apparent by 1963. The Nimitz Freeway runs diagonally through the left center. Look for an arrowhead-shaped landmass in San Leandro Bay. Arrowhead Marsh probably formed when torrential rains in 1875 breached the diversion channel and broke through the puddle wall being constructed for Chabot Dam. The raging waters carried 20,000 yards of debris downstream. (San Leandro Museum.)

EAST FOURTEENTH STREET AND MARIO'S, 1964. Mario's Shoe Shine Parlor was a gathering spot for San Leandrans who wanted to talk about what was happening in the 1960s and 1970s. Mario Polvorosa, born in Hawaii of Portuguese ancestry, served on the city council from 1965 until 1976. He was vice-mayor his last year on the council. (SLHPDC #168.)

BRIAN COPELAND. Copeland is the only African American in this eighth-grade class photograph. The Copeland family, including eight-year-old Brian, moved to San Leandro in 1972, when the population was about one-tenth of one percent African American. Now a writer, television host, radio host, and actor, Copeland wrote and performed a one-man play about his family's experiences with racism and his personal struggles for identity in San Leandro, where he still lives. *Not a Genuine Black Man: Or, How I Claimed My Piece of Ground in the Lily-White Suburbs* became a long-running hit in San Francisco and was also performed in New York and in theaters around California. It was the basis for a book of the same title published in 2006. Both were widely praised for their striking combination of powerful emotion, great humor, and social insight. The Copeland family was at the forefront of demographic change. By the year 2000, San Leandro was 51.3-percent white, 9.9-percent African American, 23-percent Asian, and 20.1 percent who identified themselves as Latino or Hispanic. (Brian Copeland.)

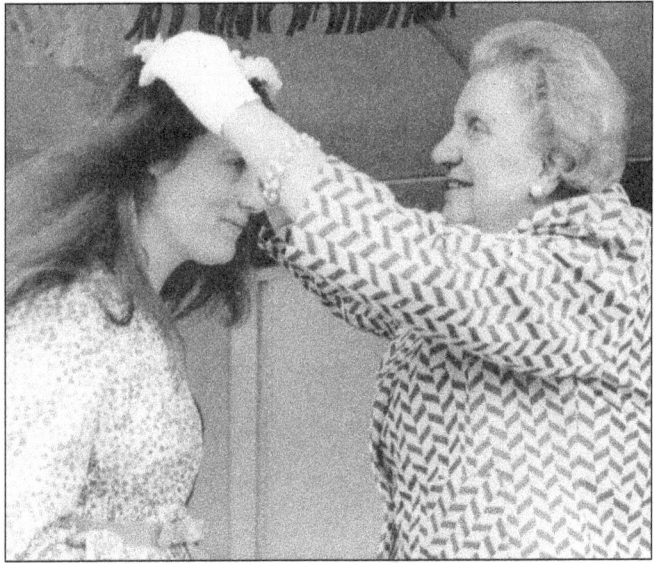

CENTENNIAL-BICENTENNIAL. Bessie Best, the 1909 cherry festival queen, crowns the 1972 queen, Ruth Phillips. Throughout 1972, San Leandro celebrated the 100th anniversary of incorporation and the 200th anniversary of the first Spanish exploration of the area. Events included a historical musical pageant, a ball, a banquet, a re-enactment of the Fages-Crespi expedition, and a cherry festival. (*San Leandro Cherry Festivals of the Past* by Ilene Herman, Courtesy City of San Leandro.)

MAYOR. Jack Maltester and a young boy admire a historic Peralta sword at a centennial celebration. Appointed mayor by the city council in 1958, Maltester became the first mayor elected by popular vote in 1962. He was re-elected three times, serving until 1978. During his tenure, the marina and shoreline were developed, a new library was built, and the Bay Area Rapid Transit extended its line through the town. (SLHPDC #2289.)

CASA PERALTA. John and Barbara Mathews Brooks bought this historic home and donated it to the city of San Leandro in 1972. From left to right are Mayor Jack Maltester, Barbara Mathews Brooks, John Brooks, William Suerstedt, Mario Polvorosa, Gregory Pomares, Al Nahm, Alvin Kant, and Gunner Seymon. Now a historic house museum, it combines the stories of Spanish/Mexican California and a wealthy Peralta descendant in the 1920s. (SLHPDC #1836.)

BILL LOCKYER. Lockyer is second from left in this photograph of the San Leandro School Board, which was his first elected office. Lockyer attended elementary through high school in San Leandro. He served for 25 years in the California legislature, including six years as president pro tempore of the senate. He was then elected California attorney general, where he served from 1999 to 2006. He is currently the state treasurer. (Bill Lockyer.)

FRIENDS OF THE SAN LEANDRO CREEK (FSLC). Recognizing an essential and irreplaceable natural resource, the FSLC organized in 1993 to protect and restore San Leandro Creek. The members organize twice-yearly creek cleanups, hold a Watershed Awareness Festival every spring, collect data on water quality and other creek information, and raise funds to create a San Leandro Watershed Education Center. These two photographs depict segments of *Nature's Hidden Treasure*, a mural painted under the bridge over San Leandro Creek at Root Park. Muralist Veronica Lacarra Werckmeister incorporated the winning drawing from San Leandro High School art classes with aspects from other entries for the final design. She worked with more than 100 volunteers to create the 19,500-square-foot mural in 1998. (Both, FSLC.)

SAN LEANDRO PUBLIC LIBRARY. In 1997, the library moved to temporary quarters on Alvarado Street while a major retrofit and renovation expanded the Main Library. The beautiful facility was ready for the 21st century when it reopened on December 16, 2000, with 75,000 square feet, 75 public computers, a gift shop, and a café. San Leandro also built a new, awarding-winning library to replace the old Manor Branch. At left, three children show off their balloon creations at the summer reading program carnival, which rewards every child who finishes 10 book reports during the summer program. About 3,000 children participate. Since 1986, Youth Services Senior Librarian Penny Peck has been planning educational and fun programs, from story times to Family Fun Nights to the Heritage Fair, that bring families to celebrate books, community, and San Leandro's many cultures. (Above, author's collection; left, San Leandro Library.)

SAN LEANDRO MUSEUM AND ART GALLERY. Third-grade students dress up to enact roles from San Leandro's past while on a tour at the new local history museum that opened in 2004. About 50 classes a year visit the museum to learn about San Leandro and California history in a hands-on learning environment. The museum shares the beautiful Casa Peralta courtyard and offers an auditorium, art gallery, and San Leandro history exhibits. Building the new museum for future generations and teaching children about San Leandro's past exemplifies the city motto: "Proud of Our Past; Looking to the Future." (Author's collection.)

Visit us at
arcadiapublishing.com

www.ingramcontent.com/pod-product-compliance
Lightning Source LLC
Chambersburg PA
CBHW050550110426
42813CB00008B/2313